Summer Cook

By the same Author

Quick Cook

The Daily Telegraph Book of
Breads, Cakes & Puddings

THANE PRINCE

Summer Cook

Chatto & Windus
LONDON

First published 1994

1 3 5 7 9 10 8 6 4 2

First published in the United Kingdom in 1994 by
Chatto & Windus Limited
Random House, 20 Vauxhall Bridge Road, London SW1V 2SA

Random House Australia (Pty) Limited
20 Alfred Street, Milson's Point, Sydney
New South Wales 2061, Australia

Random House New Zealand Limited
18 Poland Road, Glenfield
Auckland 10, New Zealand

Random House South Africa (Pty) Limited
PO Box 337, Bergvlei, South Africa

Random House UK Limited Reg. No. 954009

A CIP catalogue record for this book is
available from the British Library

ISBN 0 7011 4893 4

Designed by Clive Dorman
Typeset by Clive Dorman & Co.

Printed and bound in Great Britain by
Butler & Tanner Ltd, Frome and London

CONTENTS

For my mother Mona Hurry, with love

ACKNOWLEDGEMENTS

Once again I have more people to thank than I can list by name, but some who must be mentioned are:

My husband, Bob and daughters, Jade and Amber who put up with me always saying I'd be there in a minute and then disappearing for hours.

My sister Maureen Seiden who helped put the book together, Rowena Skelton-Wallace of Chatto & Windus who sent encouraging postcards and Madeleine David who painted the lovely watercolours.

Tim Rostron and Will Ellsworth-Jones of the *Telegraph* Weekend section and Jacqueline Korn my agent, who are ever supportive. Chefs and colleages, who generously answered my endless questions.

And finally Vlad the Hamster, who shared my long winter vigil in the basement while I typed the manuscript.

INTRODUCTION

When I sat down to write this book I was filled with thoughts of summer meals I have enjoyed – sun-drenched and, this being England, wind-whipped, meals shared with family and friends or eaten alone in my garden.

There is something nostalgic about summer food. I remember when picnics on the white sanded north Norfolk beaches were a regular treat. We would walk down the long cliff path and then far along the beach to find a spot that met with my mother's approval, then we would settle on the sand, unpack buckets, spades, windbreaks and shrimping nets and our picnic: loaves of bread, pots of jam, apples, cheese and flasks of tea.

It was on these picnics that I learned to catch shrimps, hook crabs out from under the rocks in the tidal pools and pick samphire from the nearby marshes. We dug for cockles and collected mussels, then carried them home in our buckets. We boiled our catch in sea water, and burned our fingers as we peeled the hot shrimps so we could eat them, still warm, between thickly buttered slices of fresh bread.

We went to fruit farms to pick strawberries and sat, exhausted and satiated from over-eating, in the warm summer sun. We gathered mushrooms before breakfast from the meadows and cooked them in bacon fat on the Aga.

We searched in the stubble fields for ears of wheat and cracked them open with our teeth to suck out the flour within. To me scratched ankles and the first blackberries were the signs that summer was drawing to a close.

Since that enchanted time I have tasted summer in many different parts of the world. I have breakfasted on a beach overlooking Sydney harbour, lunched at tiny street-side cafés in Paris where the sun always seems to shine, and celebrated 200 years of American independence at a Fourth of July barbecue in New Jersey. One memorable evening we dined in a ruined palace on a hilltop in Tuscany – the occasion was a barrel rolling festival in Montepulciano – and though I speak no Italian we ate, drank, danced and laughed the night away.

Each of these memorable meals has in some way coloured this book. Summer is an open, generous time, a time of plenty and of warmth, and this book will, I hope, bring you as much delight and pleasure as the food in it has given me.

SOUPS &
STARTERS

I often think the best way to start a meal on a warm summer's night is to sip chilled wine and eat something very simple. A plate of Parma ham or finely sliced salami, some fresh ripe figs, Charentais melon filled with pineau, or grilled vegetables are all favourites. Eaten out of doors, food takes on new exciting flavours and sitting amid the perfumed air of the garden there seems to be a touch of magic at the feast.

But we live in the real world and must consider the vagaries of the summer weather. More times than I care to remember I have had a carefully planned meal for a summer's night put into jeopardy by the fickleness of the climate. So if the temperature looks a little unsettled I try to include a soup, to be served either hot or cold, so there is a warming beginning to the meal if a sudden chill settles on the garden.

Everyone feels hungrier when eating out of doors. With sharpened appetites plus the tantalizing smell of food cooking over charcoal and the uncertain timing of a barbecue it's a good idea to have plenty of fresh bread on hand to keep hunger pangs at bay.

WATERCRESS SOUP

This is surely the simplest of summer soups. Keep it chilled in the fridge and if the storm clouds gather you can heat it to boiling point just before serving.

SERVES 4

1 tablespoon olive oil
2 shallots, finely chopped
450 g (1 lb) old potatoes, peeled and cubed
225 g (8 oz) watercress, roughly chopped
600 ml (1 pint) chicken stock
sea salt and black pepper
140 ml (¼ pint) single cream
chopped chives

In a large saucepan heat the oil and fry the shallots for 4-5 minutes until soft but not brown. Add the potatoes to the pan and cook for 2-3 minutes. Now put in half the watercress, and the stock. Bring to the boil and simmer for 8-10 minutes or until the potatoes are just tender.

Pour the mixture into a food processor or blender and process until smooth. Tip half the soup into a clean pan and add the remaining watercress to the blender. Process well until the cress is finely chopped. Stir it into the soup in the pan and bring to the boil. Cook for 1 minute. Taste and correct the seasoning, adding extra water if the flavour of the soup seems too intense but remembering that you will be adding cream later.

Pour the soup into a bowl and chill.

To serve cold, swirl the cream into the soup and sprinkle with chives. To serve hot, warm the soup just to boiling point, add the cream and garnish with chives.

GREEN PEA AND MINT SOUP

This beautiful summer soup captures the flavour of that most fleeting of crops, tiny garden peas. If you don't have a bountiful garden use frozen petits pois and lots of freshly picked mint.

If you intend to serve the soup hot, use butter to make it as this will give a wonderful flavour. If there is the slightest chance you will want to serve it chilled I suggest you use a good light olive oil. Chilled butter will form tiny globules, giving a less than perfect texture.

SERVES 8

60 g (2 oz) butter or 4 tablespoons light oil
1 medium onion, chopped
900 g (2 lb) podded peas
1 bunch fresh mint, roughly chopped
1 teaspoon salt
1 teaspoon sugar
1.5 litres (2½ pints) good chicken or vegetable stock
crème fraîche or single cream

Melt the butter or heat the oil in a deep saucepan. Add the onion and cook until it softens, taking care not to brown the onion or let the butter burn.

Now add the peas and the mint, reserving a few small leaves for the garnish. Allow the mixture to stew gently in the butter for about 5 minutes, stirring often.

Add the salt, sugar and stock and bring to the boil. Simmer for 10 minutes, then remove from the heat and process in a liquidizer until smooth. Pour the blended soup through a sieve, pressing down to push through as much liquid as possible.

Serve hot, or allow the soup to cool, then chill. Garnish with a swirl of crème fraîche and the reserved mint leaves.

GAZPACHO

Spanish farmworkers drink great bowls of gazpacho to sustain them, as it refreshes and nourishes when the weather is too hot for serious eating.

If I want to make this soup quickly, or I can't find ripe tomatoes, I use a carton of good quality tomato juice to replace them.

SERVES 6

2 thick slices country-style day-old white bread
2 tablespoons warm water
3-4 tablespoons good Spanish olive oil
1 tablespoon red wine vinegar
1 large Spanish onion
2 cloves garlic, crushed
sea salt and black pepper
1 green pepper, cut in half
1 cucumber, cut in half
6-8 large ripe tomatoes or 600 ml (1 pint) tomato juice
275 ml (½ pint) iced water

Break up the bread and place in a large bowl, add the warm water and stir well. When the bread is mushy add the olive oil and vinegar.

Grate the onion into the bowl and add the garlic. Season with a little salt and pepper and stir well. Peel half the pepper and half the cucumber with a potato peeler or sharp knife. Grate them into the bowl.

Put the tomatoes in a separate bowl and cover with boiling water. Slip off the skins then cut the tomatoes open. Scoop out the seeds and cut out any hard core. Place the tomato flesh in a blender with the iced water and whizz until the tomatoes are finely chopped. Add to the bowl. Stir everything together, adding enough extra iced water to give the desired consistency. The soup can be served very thin or almost sliceable, but the flavour should never be watery. Taste and correct seasoning.

Finely dice the unpeeled half cucumber and pepper and use to garnish the soup. Chill until needed.

WHITE GAZPACHO

Most people think of gazpacho as the robustly flavoured mixture just described, but there are almost as many recipes for this Spanish soup as there are people who make it. This elegant version is lighter in flavour.

SERVES 4

85 g (3 oz) 2-day-old white bread without crusts
600 ml (1 pint) milk and water mixed
2 hardboiled eggs
85 g (3 oz) blanched almonds
2 plump cloves fresh garlic
salt and white pepper
140 ml (¼ pint) light olive oil
1-2 tablespoons sherry vinegar
½ cucumber, peeled and diced
2 tablespoons fresh chives, chopped

Put the bread to soak in ¼ of the milk and water mixture. Place the egg yolks, almonds, garlic and seasoning in a processor and process until you have a smooth paste. With the motor running add the oil as if you were making mayonnaise, slowly at first then a little more quickly, in a thin stream.

Now add the soaked bread, keeping the motor running. Thin the soup with the remaining milk and water, seasoning to taste with sherry vinegar, salt and pepper.

Chill and serve garnished with finely chopped egg white, the cucumber and chives.

Iced tomato soup

You really need an electric ice cream churn to freeze the soup perfectly, otherwise just serve well chilled, diluted to taste with water.

SERVES 4

**2 slices fresh white bread
2 tablespoons olive oil
1 tablespoon wine vinegar
600 ml (1 pint) tomato juice
½ Spanish onion, finely grated
½ red pepper, peeled and finely grated
10 cm (4 inch) piece cucumber, peeled and finely grated
1 tablespoon vodka
Tabasco
salt and pepper
fresh coriander to garnish**

Break up the bread, then whizz in a food processor with the oil and vinegar. Now add the remaining ingredients and process until well mixed. Season to taste. Pour the mixture into an electric ice cream churn and freeze until the ice is ready. You will need to stop the machine from time to time and scrape down the sides to stop uneven freezing.

Serve spooned into glasses and garnished with coriander.

Deep-fried courgette flowers

One of the glorious memories of my first visit to Florence was a dish of these golden crisp-fried courgette flowers eaten at an open-air restaurant. Pick the flowers when they are just open and check the insides for insects. Don't wash the flowers unless absolutely necessary. As they wilt very quickly cook soon after picking as possible.

SERVES 4

**about 12 very fresh courgette flowers
60 g (2 oz) plain flour
water to mix
sea salt and black pepper
olive oil for deep-frying
lemon wedges**

Make a batter about the consistency of single cream with the flour and water. Season well. Heat the oil and when hot dip the flowers into the batter, drain off the excess and then fry, over a moderate heat, until golden brown, turning once if necessary. Drain on absorbent paper and serve with wedges of lemon.

COURGETTE AND GARDEN HERB SUMMER SOUP

Vichyssoise is one of the most popular cold soups, but leeks, an essential ingredient, are hard to find in midsummer. And why use out-of-season leeks when there are so many other wonderful vegetables to choose from? I've chosen courgettes for this potato-based soup. You can stir in a little single cream before serving, but I think it masks the light, fresh taste of the summer herbs. I like French tarragon or marjoram but summer savory or chives are also delicious.

SERVES 4

**1 tablespoon light olive oil
1 medium shallot, finely chopped
285 g (10 oz) old potatoes (peeled weight), cubed
1 litre (1½ pints) vegetable or chicken stock
450 g (1 lb) small firm courgettes
2 tablespoons chopped fresh herbs
sea salt and black pepper**

Heat the oil in a saucepan and fry the shallot over a medium heat until it softens. Add the potatoes and toss in the hot oil. Pour on the stock, bring to the boil and simmer until soft, about 10 minutes.

Liquidize the mixture and return to the saucepan. Grate the courgettes, discarding any juices that collect, and add to the soup. Bring to the boil and simmer for 2 minutes. Cool and then chill.

About 1 hour before serving stir in your chosen herbs and correct the seasoning.

DEEP-FRIED
STUFFED COURGETTE FLOWERS

These courgette flowers would make a tasty light supper dish for 2 or a starter for 4.

SERVES 2 OR 4

115 g (4 oz) cottage cheese
8 fresh courgette flowers (see page 15)
30 g (1 oz) freshly grated parmesan cheese
30 g (1 oz) smoked ham
2 tablespoons chopped parsley
1 small clove garlic
sea salt and black pepper
oil for deep-frying

FOR THE BATTER
60 g (2 oz) plain flour
salt and pepper
water to mix

Make the batter by mixing the flour with enough water to give a smooth cream. Season well.

Drain the cottage cheese well, put into a food processor with the other stuffing ingredients, and process to a paste.

Gently open each flower and divide the stuffing between them. Close the flowers carefully.

Heat the oil. When it's hot, dip each flower into the batter, drain off the excess and fry until golden brown. Serve at once.

CHICKEN CONSOMMÉ WITH CHILLI AND FRESH CORIANDER

Eating highly spiced food is cooling. I learned this in Mexico on an overwhelmingly humid day when there was no air-conditioning in our hotel and the pool looked like a bowl of lime jelly. The soup we were served was piping hot and thick with chopped coriander and chillies. Back in England I make a less fiery version that refreshes in our milder climate.

SERVES 4

1 chicken carcass (raw is best)
1 tablespoon oil
1 large onion
2 carrots
1 leek
2 sticks celery
parsley stems
salt and black pepper
fresh green chillies, seeded and finely chopped
1 bunch fresh green coriander, chopped

First make a concentrated chicken stock. Chop the carcass into smallish bits and place in a pan with a little chicken fat if you have it, or 1 tablespoon oil. Fry the bones until coloured and then add the unpeeled, washed, chopped vegetables and the parsley stems and fry until lightly coloured. Add seasoning and just enough water to cover. Stir well and simmer for 30 minutes, adding more water as necessary.

Strain the stock into a clean pan and taste. If the mixture is too strong, dilute it; if too light, boil over a high heat to reduce. Just before serving correct the seasoning, stir in the chillies and coriander.

Avocado, mozzarella and tomato crostini

Serving tasty morsels on toasted bread is an idea from Italy that has been embraced by many fashionable restaurants.

To tell if an avocado is ripe, cradle the fruit in the palm of your hand and press it gently. It should yield slightly. Fruit with obvious skin blemishes should be avoided as the flesh may be black when cut. The tendency for avocado to blacken means that lemon juice must be painted on to all cut surfaces to preserve the colour.

Serves 4

**4 large slices white country-style French or Italian bread
4 tablespoons olive oil
1 large clove garlic, peeled
1 large or 2 small ripe avocados
8 sun-dried tomato halves in oil
1 mozzarella cheese, sliced
fresh basil or flat-leaf parsley
sea salt and black pepper**

Heat the grill and lightly toast the bread on both sides. Keeping the toast on the grill pan, drizzle over half the oil. Cut the garlic clove and rub over the toast.

Peel, stone and slice the avocados and arrange on the toast along with the sun-dried tomato. Divide the mozzarella between the crostini and put some fresh herb leaves on each one. Season with salt and pepper and drizzle over the remaining oil. Cook under a very hot grill until the cheese melts and browns. Serve at once.

AVOCADO MOUSSE WITH TOMATO SALSA

This very pretty mousse must be kept closely covered until it is needed to prevent discoloration. You could garnish it with a few prawns or scallops.

SERVES 4-6

1 sachet powdered gelatine
200 ml (⅓ pint) good chicken stock
2 large ripe avocados
juice of 1 lemon
200 ml (⅓ pint) single cream
Tabasco and sea salt
1 tablespoon chopped chives

FOR THE SALSA

4-6 ripe tomatoes
1 shallot, finely chopped
½ fresh green chilli
juice of lemon or lime to taste
sea salt and black pepper
2 tablespoons chopped fresh coriander

At least 2 hours before serving, make the mousse. Sprinkle the gelatine powder over the stock and leave to swell for 5 minutes. Warm the stock until the gelatine dissolves, then allow to cool.

In a blender, process the avocado flesh, lemon juice and cream until smooth. Add the gelatine and season to taste with Tabasco and salt. Stir in the chives.

Pour the mixture into a ring mould or 6 individual ramekins, tapping each one sharply on the work top so any air bubbles come to the surface. Cover with film and chill until needed.

Meanwhile, make the salsa. Skin the tomatoes by dipping in boiling water for 60 seconds. Remove the seeds and then chop the flesh. Add the shallot, chilli and lemon or lime juice to the tomato. Season and stir in the coriander.

Allow to sit for 30 minutes to let the flavours develop. Turn the mousse out on to a serving dish or plates and spoon over a little salsa.

Avocado, feta and melon salad with mint dressing

Choose perfectly ripe avocados and the most scented melon you can find for this recipe. Prepare just prior to serving with crusty bread.

Serves 4-6

**2 large ripe avocados
juice of ½ lemon
225 g (8 oz) feta cheese, cubed
1 ripe, scented melon
1 handful chopped mint leaves
salad leaves to garnish**

For the dressing
**4 tablespoons light olive oil
1 tablespoon white wine vinegar
sea salt and black pepper
¼ teaspoon sugar**

Peel the avocados and remove the stones, cut the flesh into cubes and sprinkle with lemon juice. Add the feta. Remove all the seeds and skin from the melon and cut into cubes. Mix with the avocado and cheese and toss in the mint.

Place all the dressing ingredients in a screw-topped jar and shake until well combined. Pour over the salad and divide between individual serving plates. Garnish with a few small salad leaves.

TAPÉNADE

I like the ingredients for this olive spread to be roughly chopped to go with the robust flavour, but you can purée everything if you like, to make a smooth cream. Serve on thin pitta toasts, French bread, rusks or even as a sauce with freshly cooked pasta or hardboiled eggs.

115 g (4 oz) plump, stoned black olives
1 small tin anchovy fillets in oil
1 tablespoon pickled capers
2 plump cloves garlic
140 ml (¼ pint) good olive oil
sea salt and black pepper

Using a pestle and mortar mash the ingredients together, adding salt and pepper to taste.

Let the tapénade sit for at least 1 hour before serving to allow the flavours to develop.

DEEP-FRIED RISOTTO BALLS STUFFED WITH MOZZARELLA

This unusual party dish can be made with half quantities of any of the risotto recipes later in the book, leaving out the courgette flowers or other large ingredients. It is also a wonderful way of using up leftover risotto.

SERVES 4

1 ball mozzarella cheese
1 tablespoon finely chopped chives and parsley
about 340 g (12 oz) cooked, cold risotto
225 g (8 oz) stale white breadcrumbs
oil for deep-frying
freshly grated parmesan to serve

Cut the mozzarella into 1 cm (½ inch) cubes. Mix the herbs into the risotto. Taking just less than a tablespoon at a time, make the mixture into balls, burying a cube of cheese in each one.

Roll the balls in the breadcrumbs and place in a single layer to rest for about 30 minutes.

Heat the oil and fry the risotto balls until golden. Drain on absorbent paper. Keep warm in a low oven until all the balls have been fried.

Serve warm, generously dusted with parmesan, as canapés or as a starter or a light meal with a green salad.

WEED SOUP

One April I was staying in the lovely West Town of Kinsdale. I had been attending a food forum where the best of Irish produce was on show. The delegates spoke of international markets and global food policies, but what a delight it was to eat one evening at the Old Presbytery, a small guest house run by Ken and Cathleen Buggy, and dine on foods that had quite literally come from their own back garden. It was here that I first sampled weed soup.

When cooking with weeds use the topmost, tender leaves. Always consult a reliable guide to make sure they are edible, and avoid any you are not sure of. For this soup I would use wild garlic, sorrel, nettles and dandelion leaves. Watercress and young spinach may also be used.

SERVES 4

2 tablespoons light olive oil
1 medium onion, finely chopped
450 g (1 lb) old potatoes, peeled and diced
1 litre (1½ pints) chicken stock
about 450 g (1 lb) mixed edible weeds
140 ml (¼ pint) single cream (optional)
salt and pepper

Heat the oil in a large saucepan and cook the onion slowly until it softens and becomes transparent. Turn the potatoes in the hot oil for about 2 minutes, add the stock and simmer for 5 minutes.

Wash and pat dry the weeds, removing any hard stems. Chop roughly and add to the soup. Simmer for 3-4 minutes, then pour the contents into a food processor and whizz until smooth.

Return to a clean pan and bring back to the boil. Add cream and season to taste. Don't boil the soup once the added.

AUBERGINE FRITTERS
WITH YOGHURT

Fresh young aubergines do not need salting before cooking. If you are not certain about the age of your aubergine, sprinkle the slices with salt and leave to drain for about 45 minutes, then rinse well and dry thoroughly on kitchen paper.

SERVES 4

**600 ml (1 pint) thick natural yoghurt
1 teaspoon ground cumin
1 teaspoon ground coriander
2 medium aubergines
60 g (2 oz) plain flour
½ teaspoon celery salt
1-2 eggs, beaten
olive oil for shallow-frying
fresh coriander leaves and lemon wedges for serving**

Beat the yoghurt until smooth and pour into a serving dish. Sprinkle on the spices and chill until needed.

Cut the aubergines into thick slices. Mix the flour with the celery salt on a plate. Beat 1 egg with salt in a wide, shallow bowl. Reserve the second egg to use if necessary.

Heat the oil in a large shallow pan. Dip the slices of aubergine first in the egg and then in the flour, giving each one a light coating. Fry the slices, a few at a time, turning as necessary until they are light golden brown on both sides. Drain on absorbent paper and keep hot while you continue to fry the rest.

Serve the fritters very hot with lemon wedges, garnished with fresh coriander and a spoonful of yoghurt.

FEUILLETÉ OF ASPARAGUS

Even the thought of asparagus makes me feel slightly decadent – it must be the glorious flavour, wonderful melting quality and all that delicious butter. I usually serve asparagus with hollandaise sauce this or quite simply with melted butter and lemon juice. Last year I ate asparagus in Italy dipping the spears into a mixture of green olive oil sharpened with a few drops of balsamic vinegar. I also discovered a wonderful asparagus risotto which can be made by simply adapting the recipe for courgette risotto (page 99), but if I want to do something a little more sophisticated with the very thin sprue asparagus I like this elegant dish. The pastry cases can be made the day before.

SERVES 4

340 g (12 oz) ready-made puff pastry
beaten egg to glaze
450 g (1 lb) sprue asparagus (cleaned weight)
1 small shallot, very finely chopped
140 ml (¼ pint) dry white wine
2 tablespoons white wine vinegar
1 generous tablespoon double cream
140 g (5 oz) butter, diced
salt and white pepper

Roll out the pastry until it forms a 25 cm (10 inch) x 12 cm (5 inch) rectangle. Cut into four equal rectangles and score the tops with a sharp knife to make a diamond pattern. Brush with egg to glaze and place on a baking sheet. Cook in a preheated oven at 220°C/425°F/Gas 7 for 10-15 minutes, or until well risen and golden brown. Remove from the oven, allow to cool, then slice off the tops and remove any uncooked dough from the centres.

Bring a large saucepan of very lightly salted water to the boil and about 4 minutes before you wish to serve the dish cook the sprue. The best way to tell if asparagus is cooked is by the smell. Drain and keep warm. Reheat the pastry cases.

To make the sauce, cook the shallot in the wine and vinegar in a heavy-bottomed saucepan until the mixture has almost completely evaporated and only about 2 tablespoons of liquid remain. Add the cream and as soon as it boils, turn off the heat. Add the butter all at once and whisk furiously with a balloon whisk until the sauce thickens and amalgamates. Season to taste.

To serve, place the bottom halves of the pastry cases on individual warmed plates and divide the asparagus between them. Spoon over the sauce and top with the pastry lids.

ARTICHOKE HEARTS WITH GRILLED GOATS CHEESE AND WALNUTS

Use this recipe when artichokes are at the height of their season and you won't feel so bad about throwing away all the leaves.

SERVES 4

juice of 1 lemon
4 large artichokes
225 g (8 oz) medium mature goats cheese
30 g (1 oz) finely chopped walnuts

FOR THE DRESSING
2 tablespoons red wine or fruit vinegar
4 tablespoons light olive oil
sea salt and black pepper
1 tablespoon finely chopped chives

Put the lemon juice into a medium saucepan and half fill with water. Using a small sharp knife trim the stems of the artichokes level with the base and cut off the leaves about 2.5 cm (1 inch) above it. Pull any remaining leaves from the base and scrape the choke away with a spoon. Rinse under cold water to remove any last pieces of the choke and then put into the saucepan. The artichoke hearts will go brown if not plunged into acidulated water.

When all the hearts have been prepared, bring the water to the boil and simmer for about 15 minutes or until they are tender but not mushy. Drain and allow to cool.

Slice the goats cheese into rounds about 5 mm (¼ inch) thick and place them on the artichoke hearts on a grill pan. Season well.

Mix the dressing ingredients in a screw-topped jar and shake to blend. The dish can be prepared up to this point and kept for several hours until needed.

Heat the grill. When the grill is hot, cook the goats cheese-covered hearts until the cheese melts, bubbles and browns. Dish up on to individual plates and spoon over a little dressing. Sprinkle on some walnuts and serve at once with French bread.

PRAWN-STUFFED ARTICHOKES

This recipe is filling enough to make a good light lunch.

SERVES 4

4 large artichokes
1 tablespoon lemon juice
115 g (4 oz) butter
2 shallots, finely chopped
1 plump clove garlic, finely chopped
170 g (6 oz) soft brown breadcrumbs
grated rind and juice of 1 lemon
2-3 tablespoons chopped parsley
sea salt and black pepper
dash of Tabasco
225 g (8 oz) cooked prawns, roughly chopped

FOR THE DRESSING
6 tablespoons olive oil
2 tablespoons wine vinegar
1-2 tablespoons lemon juice
sea salt and black pepper
1 tablespoon chopped chervil or flat-leaf parsley

Wash the artichokes well and slice about 2.5 cm (1 inch) from the top of each one. Brush the cut surfaces with lemon juice as you work. Bring a large pan of water to the boil and simmer the artichokes for 30-40 minutes, or until a knife inserted in the base goes in easily. Drain and allow to cool.

When cold, gently ease out the leaves and when you get to the centre, remove the small leaves covering the choke and finally the choke itself. Arrange the artichoke hearts in a deep sided ovenproof dish.

Melt all but 30 g (1 oz) butter and fry the shallots and garlic until soft and beginning to brown. Now mix in the breadcrumbs, lemon juice and rind, parsley, seasoning and Tabasco.

Melt the remaining butter in a frying pan and cook the prawns over a very high heat until any liquid has been driven off. Mix these into the stuffing.

Divide the stuffing between the artichoke hearts. Cover the dish with foil. Mix the dressing ingredients together in a screw-topped jar.

Thirty minutes before serving, reheat the dish at 180°C /360°F/Gas 4, and serve hot with a ramekin of dressing.

JELLIED TOMATO SALAD

This is a wonderfully light refreshing jelly. You can fill the centre of the ring with cubes of marinated feta cheese, prawns or mozzarella and avocado.

SERVES 4

1 sachet gelatine powder
4 tablespoons water
600 ml (1 pint) tomato juice
Tabasco and celery salt
1 tablespoon wine vinegar
4 spring onions, finely sliced
½ small green pepper, diced
½ cucumber, diced
fresh basil leaves

Sprinkle the gelatine powder over the water and allow to swell. Season the tomato juice to taste with Tabasco and celery salt and add the vinegar. Warm the gelatine over a bowl of hot water and when fully dissolved stir into the tomato juice.

Add the onions, pepper and cucumber to the tomato mixture. Pour into a deep ring mould and refrigerate until set.

To serve, dip the mould into hot water for about 15 seconds and invert on to a serving dish. Decorate with fresh basil leaves.

WARM GOATS CHEESE SALAD WITH RASPBERRY VINEGAR

This is a very pretty and unusual warm salad that comes from California.

SERVES 4

6 tablespoons olive oil
2 medium red onions, sliced into fine rings
4 tablespoons raspberry vinegar
sea salt and black pepper
2 tablespoons fresh white breadcrumbs
4 x 2 cm (¾ inch) thick slices medium matured goats cheese
a little olive oil for frying
selection of small salad leaves
60 g (2 oz) shelled pistachio nuts, roughly chopped

Heat 1 tablespoon oil in a frying pan and cook the onions until limp. Add the raspberry vinegar and simmer for 1 minute. Remove the onions from the pan with a slotted spoon and pour the pan juices into a screw-topped jar. Add the remaining oil and season to taste, making a dressing.

Season the breadcrumbs and press on to both sides of the cheese slices. If your chosen cheese is a little dry brush with milk before pressing on the crumbs. Chill until needed.

When you are ready to serve the dish, heat some oil in a frying pan and cook the cheese over a high heat, turning once until the crumbs are a light golden brown.

Divide the salad leaves and onion rings between 4 plates and top each one with a piece of fried goats cheese. Sprinkle on the pistachios and drizzle over a little dressing. Serve at once.

WARM GOATS CHEESE AND HAZELNUT SALAD

I make no excuses for including another warm chevre salad as I love the combination of full flavoured warm cheese, cold bitter herb salad and oily dressing. Here some extra texture is provided by crisp fried or toasted croûtons.

SERVES 4

8 thin slices French bread
225 g (8 oz) soft fresh goats cheese
selection of bitter salad leaves, such as rocket and herbs
1 tablespoon walnut oil
3 tablespoons light olive oil
1½ tablespoons white wine vinegar
sea salt and black pepper
60 g (2 oz) chopped hazelnuts

Toast or fry the bread until golden on both sides. Divide the cheese between the toasts and place on a grill pan. Arrange the salad leaves on 4 plates. Mix the oils and vinegar together adding seasoning to taste to make the dressing.

Cook the cheese under a preheated grill until it melts and browns. Serve on the salad leaves, scattered with nuts and drizzled with dressing.

Smoked trout and chervil tartlets

SERVES 6

450 g (1 lb) shortcrust pastry
285 g (10 oz) smoked trout (boned and skinned weight)
2 size 2 eggs
275 ml (½ pint) single cream
finely grated zest of 1 lemon
sea salt and black pepper
2 tablespoons finely chopped chervil or chives

Line 6 x 12 cm (5 inch) tartlet tins with the pastry. Chill. Flake the fish and divide between the pastry cases.

Beat the eggs with the cream and lemon zest. Season and mix in the herbs. Spoon the custard over the fish and bake the tartlets in a preheated oven at 200°C/400°F/Gas 6 for 25-30 minutes, or until the pastry is cooked through and the tartlets are golden. Serve warm or cold with a mixed leaf salad.

Piquant tuna pâté

This is a wonderful standby. Press the pâté into an earthenware bowl or serve it on individual plates with a lightly dressed green salad. It goes well with hardboiled eggs as part of an hors d'oeuvre.

SERVES 4-6

400 g (14 oz) tin tuna in oil
1 tablespoon pickled capers
6 small pickled gherkins
170 g (6 oz) curd or cream cheese
sea salt, black pepper and Tabasco
lemon juice, to taste

Put all the ingredients into a food processor and process until well combined. Serve with hot toast or French bread.

WARM SALMON AND PINK GRAPEFRUIT SALAD

The delicate pinks of the salmon and grapefruit are nicely contrasted with the dark green leaves. This salad looks pretty with the fish on the leaves at one side of the plate and the fruit fanned out on the other side.

SERVES 4

450 g (1 lb) fresh salmon (skinned, boned weight)
2 pink fleshed grapefruit
salad leaves
1-2 tablespoons olive oil
30 g (1 oz) slivered hazelnuts

FOR THE DRESSING
juice of ½ grapefruit
2-3 tablespoons light olive oil
sea salt and black pepper
a little caster sugar

Cut the salmon into 2.5 cm (1 inch) cubes. Using a sharp knife cut all the peel and pith from the grapefruit and remove the segments. Arrange these as described above on 4 plates, with the salad leaves on the plates also. Mix the dressing ingredients together, tasting and correcting the seasoning.

Heat the oil in a large pan and fry the salmon cubes over a medium high heat until they are cooked through. The flesh should be just opaque. Remove from the pan and place on the salad leaves. Turn up the heat and quickly fry the hazelnuts until they brown. Scatter over the salmon and drizzle on the dressing.

POTTED SHRIMPS

This once popular English dish seems to have fallen out of fashion and I seldom see it now on restaurant menus. I am sure part of the problem is the time it takes to peel the little brown shrimps, but they have such a wonderful flavour that the end result is well worth the effort.

SERVES 4

1.2 litres (2 pints) boiled shrimps
about 225 g (8 oz) butter
sea salt and black pepper
ground mace

Peel the shrimps carefully. Heat 60 g (2 oz) butter in a pan and add the prepared shrimps. Season to taste with salt, pepper and mace, remembering that the seasoning will not taste as strong when the dish is chilled. Stir well to coat, and warm through for 1-2 minutes. Divide the shrimps between 4 small ramekin dishes, pressing down lightly.

Heat the remaining butter and pour into a jug, leaving the lees behind. Pour this clarified butter over the shrimps to cover completely. Chill overnight, then turn out and serve with thin slices of brown bread and butter and fresh lemon wedges.

RILLETTES

Rillettes are a traditional dish from central France. Fat pork is slowly roasted, then shredded and potted in its fat to give a rich tasty pâté.

SERVES 4

1.3 kg (3 lb) fat belly of pork, cubed
2 sprigs fresh thyme
1 teaspoon sea salt
black pepper
¼ teaspoon quatre épices or spice mix
4 tablespoons water

Put the pork in a heavy-lidded casserole with the remaining ingredients. Cook in a preheated oven, at 160°C/350°F/Gas 4, for about 4 hours, until the meat is very tender.

Drain the meat and cut away any skin and bones. Using 2 forks, pull the meat into fine shreds, season again with a little salt and pepper and pack into a sterilized pot. Allow the fat to separate from any remaining juices. Reheat the fat and pour a thick layer over the meat. Cool and refrigerate for 2-3 days, then serve with crusty bread or toast.

PARMA HAM WITH FIGS

This is so simple, it can't be called a recipe. The classic combination of figs and prosciutto, the raw, cured ham from the north of Italy, is found countrywide when the lush purple figs are in season.

I recently visited Parma and saw for myself the amazing storehouses where the ham is cured. The process is very simple, but strictly controlled and monitored. The hams are salted twice, then washed and dried, and hung in a cool dry atmosphere for at least 12 months. The end result is a wonderfully pink, creamy textured ham with a soft, sweet flavour. True Parma ham is always marked with a crown, branded on to the skin of the whole ham or marked on packages if you buy it sliced.

I was able to try ham freshly sliced from the bone as well as that packed in the latest vacuum packs. Go for the vacuum packs if sales are slack in your local delicatessen. It tastes freshly cut and is far superior to the slightly oxidized ham from a less busy shop.

Full flavoured, scented melons such as Charentais or Galia are a delicious substitute for figs. When choosing melons, press them very gently with your fingers if you like, but the best test of a melon's ripeness is its smell. If the scent is rich and heady the melon is ripe, if there is little or no scent there may be little or no flavour, and if the scent has a slightly fermented tang the melon may be past its best.

Flakes of freshly cut parmesan cheese are as delicious served with figs or melon as the regional ham.

Allow at least 2 figs and 2-3 slices of ham per person. If your budget will allow it, be generous; I have never had leftovers when serving these delicious foods.

FISH

When I started planning this chapter I soon realised that every fish recipe I chose seemed to shout out that this was summer food at its best. Family holidays in Suffolk and France buying fish fresh from the boat have meant that the freshest and simplest of our holiday food has been pan-fried fish seasoned with a few garden herbs and some sea salt. Eaten with bread, fresh from the baker, such uncomplicated meals are often the most memorable.

Some fish is seasonal; wild salmon for instance, is at its best during the summer months; but much is available all year round, and often there is much greater choice at this time of year as fishing boats do not have to contend with rough winter seas.

In Britain, for some reason, we tend not to eat shellfish such as mussels and oysters unless there is an 'r' in the month but a short trip to northern France will quickly show that mussels can be eaten all year round without ill effect. Because the flatter, slower growing native oysters breed in the summer months they are not available between April and September, but cupped Pacific oysters can be eaten throughout the year.

There is no best way to cook fish. You must simply choose the freshest fish available. You can steam, grill, poach or pan fry it, but remember that most fish cooks quickly and should be served once the flesh is just opaque. Over-cooked, dry fibrous fish brings back horrible memories of my own school dinners and should be avoided at all costs!

POACHED SALMON

Salmon makes an easily prepared and delicious party meal. The crucial thing is not whether the salmon is farmed or wild, but how the fish is cooked. Overcooked salmon tastes strongly of fish oil, and is either pappy or rock solid. But lightly poached or baked salmon is quite delightful and feeds the five thousand with ease.

The best way to cook a whole fish is in a fish kettle. Simply place the fish in the kettle, cover with cold water, and throw in some sliced onion, peppercorns, coarse salt, bay leaves and lemon slices. Put on the lid and bring the water up to boiling point. Allow the fish to simmer for 1 minute and then turn off the heat. Allow the fish to sit in the water for 30 minutes if serving hot, or until cooled if serving cold.

If you are serving the fish hot, lift it out on the kettle tray, remove the upper skin, and invert the fish on to a plate. You can now remove the lower skin, give the plate a quick wipe and decorate it with some lemon or watercress. Nothing could be simpler.

FILLETS OF SALMON WITH BALSAMIC VINEGAR

If you have a plentiful supply of wild salmon use it for this dish as the leaner fish takes the taste of oil and vinegar well. Otherwise use lean tail fillets of good farmed salmon. As you really do need 2 tablespoons of balsamic vinegar, use one of the brands readily available in supermarkets.

SERVES 4

2 tablespoons olive oil
4 fillets of salmon, skinned and boned
2 tablespoons balsamic vinegar
sea salt and black pepper

Heat the oil in a pan large enough to take all the fish fillets in a single layer. Cook the fish over a high heat, turning once, until lightly browned on both sides and cooked through. This will take 6-8 minutes.

Remove the fillets from the pan and place on a heated serving dish. Pour the vinegar into the hot pan, stir well and spoon the mixture over the fish. Season and serve at once.

Wild rice and steamed spinach would be delicious with this dish.

SALMON BAKED WITH ELDERFLOWERS

This is a lovely way of using the bumper crop of elderflowers that can be gleaned from hedgerows in early summer.

SERVES 4-6

1 handful fresh elderflowers
sea salt and black pepper
1 small salmon, about 900 g-1.3 kg (2-3 lb), skinned and filleted
275 ml (½ pint) white wine
60 g (2 oz) butter

Wash and gently dry the elderflowers and lay them between the lightly seasoned fillets of salmon in a greased ovenproof dish. Pour over the wine, season again and bake in a preheated oven at 180°C/360°F/Gas 4 for 20-30 minutes, basting occasionally.

Remove the cooked fish to a heated serving platter and keep warm. Pour the juices into a small saucepan and bring to the boil. Add the butter and beat with a balloon whisk until the sauce thickens slightly and is smooth.

Serve with new potatoes and tiny garden peas.

Blackened salmon

In Victorian times servants were protected by contract from having to eat salmon more than twice a week. Today this delicious fish is a luxury when caught in the wild, but farmed salmon can make a very reasonably priced summer meal. This recipe is designed to compliment the stronger taste of farmed salmon.

Serves 4

4 salmon tail fillets, skinned
1 tablespoon oil
4 tablespoons crème fraîche
lemon wedges and chopped coriander to serve

For the creole seasoning
1 tablespoon fennel seeds
1 tablespoon dried thyme
1 tablespoon dried sage
2 tablespoons dried onion flakes
2 tablespoons garlic salt
1 tablespoon black peppercorns
2 tablespoons paprika
1 teaspoon cayenne pepper

To make the Creole seasoning, place the whole spices in a well cleaned coffee grinder and whizz until finely powdered. Mix in the paprika and cayenne. (Creole seasoning may be stored in an airtight tin until needed.)

Sprinkle the seasoning on the fish and leave for about 30 minutes.

Heat the oil in a large frying pan and cook the fish over a high heat until the outside is a rich dark brown. You may need a little extra oil, but the fish will give out some.

Remove the fillets to a serving dish, add the crème fraîche to the pan and cook for 2 minutes, stirring well. Spoon this sauce over the fish and top with plenty of coriander. Serve with lemon wedges and plain rice.

SALMON CAKES WITH SORREL SAUCE

In this recipe, grated potato gives a light feel to a traditional favourite. Serve these lovely pink cakes with a creamy sauce sharpened with bitter sorrel leaves (below). If sorrel is not available use lots of fresh parsley, watercress or young spinach.

SERVES 4

450 g (1 lb) old potatoes, peeled
285 g (10 oz) fresh salmon (skinned, boned weight)
1 tablespoon chopped chives
1 tablespoon chopped tarragon
sea salt and black pepper
5-6 tablespoons olive oil for frying

Hand grate the peeled potatoes, then rinse away most of the starch under running cold water. Squeeze the potato mass in a teatowel to make it as dry as possible.

Remove all the skin and bones from the salmon, then chop finely with a sharp knife. Mix the fish, herbs and potato together, and season to taste. The mixture will be quite soft. Shape it into round cakes.

Heat the oil in a frying pan and when hot, put in the cakes. Cook over a moderate heat until the underside is golden, then turn and cook the other side. This will take 10-15 minutes.

Serve at once with sorrel sauce (below).

SORREL SAUCE

Make this sauce at the last minute, or the fresh taste of the herb will be lost.

30 g (1 oz) butter
30 g (1 oz) flour
140 ml (¼ pint) milk
140 ml (¼ pint) fish stock
handful fresh sorrel leaves
sea salt and black pepper

Mix the butter and flour in a small pan and heat to make a roux. Add the milk, beating well as the mixture thickens. Add the stock and cook until there is no taste of raw flour. Transfer the sauce to a liquidizer, add the sorrel and process until the leaves are finely chopped and the sauce is bright green.

Return it to a clean saucepan and season to taste. Simmer for 2-3 minutes to cook the sorrel, then serve.

Pan-fried trout with hazelnuts and blackberry vinegar

You could just as easily use raspberry or other fruit vinegars for this recipe, but the blackberry does give a wonderful colour to the sauce.

Serves 4

4 trout
sea salt and black pepper
2 tablespoons light olive oil
4 tablespoons slivered or chopped hazelnuts
4 tablespoons blackberry vinegar
60 g (2 oz) fresh blackberries or blackcurrants

Wash and dry the fish, seasoning well. Heat the oil in a large frying pan and cook the fish in a single layer until the skin is crisp on the outside and a knife inserted into the deepest part of the fish slips in easily. Remove to a serving dish and keep warm.

Put the chopped nuts into the pan and fry in what remains of the oil until they are a rich golden colour and smell very nutty. Deglaze the pan by adding the vinegar and stirring everything vigorously with a spoon, scraping up any bits that have stuck to the pan. Add the fruit and cook until they soften, season with salt and pepper and pour over the fish.

Serve at once with new potatoes and garden peas.

CRISP-FRIED TROUT WITH GINGER AND LIME

This oriental dish offers an exciting contrast of flavours and textures. It is wonderfully easy to cook – follow the instructions carefully and you will be able to eat the whole fish including the skin and bones.

SERVES 2

**1 medium trout
salt and pepper
plain flour
oil for deep-frying**

FOR THE DRESSING
**grated zest and juice of 2 limes
½ teaspoon caster sugar
2.5 cm (1 inch) piece fresh ginger, peeled and grated
2 medium carrots, grated
2 spring onions, sliced into fine strips
1 tablespoon light soy sauce
1 hot green chilli, finely sliced (optional)**

Mix the dressing ingredients and leave to stand.

Wash and dry the gutted fish and make deep cuts as far as the bone at 2.5 cm (1 inch) intervals along both sides. Season well and sprinkle all the surfaces with flour.

Heat about 5 cm (2 inches) oil in a pan large enough to take the trout, and fry until the fish is very crisp. To do this you should cook the fish for 2 minutes then remove it from the pan, reheat the oil and fry the fish for another 2 minutes. Continue to do this until the fish is very crisp and golden.

Remove the fish and drain on absorbent paper, then place on a serving dish and spoon over the dressing. Serve at once.

FILLETS OF SOLE WITH BLACK BEAN SAUCE

This wonderful recipe comes from the Mandarin Hotel in Hong Kong. It was devised by the head chef of the Man Wah restaurant, Lau Sik Kwan. Follow the instructions carefully and you will be able to eat everything, including the bones!

SERVES 2

1 large Dover sole (see below)
cornflour
oil for deep-frying

FOR THE SAUCE
1 teaspoon chopped garlic
1 teaspoon fresh ginger root, peeled and chopped
1 teaspoon black bean paste
½ teaspoon dried tangerine peel (optional)
4 tablespoons light stock
2 tablespoons dry sherry or rice wine
pinch of sugar
1 teaspoon oyster sauce

Ask the fishmonger to fillet the fish, keeping the bone intact. Dust the skeleton with cornflour and deep-fry it in oil until the bones are crisp and golden. Drain well and reserve. This can be done in advance.

Cut the fillets of sole into 2.5 cm (1 inch) strips, dust with cornflour and deep-fry in hot oil for 2 minutes. Keep warm.

For the sauce, heat 2 further tablespoons oil in a wok and sauté the garlic and ginger for 1 minute. Add the remaining sauce ingredients and cook, stirring constantly until the sauce reduces and thickens slightly. Warm the fish skeleton.

Add the strips of sole to the sauce and cook, tossing gently to coat until they are hot. Break the sole skeleton into portions, spoon on the fish and sauce and serve at once.

PLAICE ROULADES WITH TARRAGON BEURRE BLANC

This is a very elegant light summer dish cooked in parcels of greaseproof paper. If you are counting calories serve the fish with a little smetana rather than the beurre blanc suggested here.

SERVES 4

4 medium fillets of plaice, skinned and with the bones removed
1 leek
1 medium courgette
sea salt and black pepper
60 g (2 oz) very small button mushrooms, finely sliced
1 tablespoon butter
fresh tarragon

Wash and dry the fish, feeling for any missed bones with the tips of your fingers. Cut 4 x 30 cm (12 inch) squares of greaseproof paper and brush with melted butter. Wash the leek well and slice both it and the courgette into thin strips about 10 cm (4 inches) long.

Lay a fillet of plaice, skinned side up, on each square of paper and season with salt and pepper. Arrange vegetable strips on each fillet of fish, then roll up the fillets to enclose the leeks and courgettes. Divide the mushrooms between the parcels, slipping some under the fish rolls. Dot with butter, season again and add some leaves of fresh tarragon. Seal the edges of the parcels by folding and crimping tightly.

Cook the parcels in a preheated oven at 200°C/400°F/Gas 6 for 12-15 minutes. Serve with new potatoes and tarragon beurre blanc (see page 45).

TARRAGON BEURRE BLANC

This sauce is much less temperamental than hollandaise, and is made with a heavy saucepan and a balloon whisk.

1 shallot or white of leek, finely chopped
1 small glass white wine
2 tablespoons white wine vinegar
1 tablespoon double cream
115 g (4 oz) butter, diced
sea salt and white pepper
fresh tarragon leaves, chopped

Cook the shallot or leek in the wine and vinegar until all but 2 tablespoons have evaporated. Add the cream and as soon as it boils, remove the pan from the heat and whisk in the butter. Keep whisking until the sauce amalgamates and is smooth and glossy. At this stage you can sieve the sauce or blend it in a food processor, but I don't think it's really necessary. Season with salt and pepper and stir in the tarragon.

This sauce is delicious with plaice roulades (page 44), poached salmon or roast chicken.

PUDINA MAACHI

This recipe comes from Satish Arora, the Chef Culinare of the famous Taj Hotel group in India. This fish dish appeals to me very much as it combines Indian cooking with fresh summer herbs.

SERVES 4

675 g (1½ lb) fresh cod or haddock
3 plump cloves garlic, peeled and crushed
1 teaspoon powdered turmeric
1 dried red chilli, crushed
juice of 1 lemon
1 small bunch each mint, coriander and dill
2 tablespoons light olive oil

Cut the fish into 8 pieces and place in a shallow dish. Mix the garlic, turmeric, chilli and lemon juice and pour over the fish. Allow to sit for 30 minutes.

Remove the leaves from the herbs and chop them roughly. Take the fish from the marinade and roll the pieces in the chopped herbs, coating well. Arrange them in an ovenproof dish and drizzle on the oil.

Bake in the centre of a preheated oven at 200°C/400°F/Gas 6 for 20 minutes. Serve with rice or spiced sautéed potatoes.

GRILLED BRILL
WITH WARM HERB DRESSING

*A light herb-based dressing served with fish makes a good alternative to a rich sauce.
This idea from Provence gives a lift to the simplest grilled fish. I have used firm fillets
of brill, but any grilled white fish, and even freshly caught mackerel, is wonderful
cooked in this manner.*

SERVES 4

**1 red pepper
4 fillets of brill
sea salt and black pepper
4 tablespoons olive oil, plus oil for brushing
2 tablespoons light vegetable oil
2 tablespoons white wine vinegar
handful fresh basil, chervil, parsley and chives, chopped
pitted black olives**

Cut the red pepper into quarters and place under the grill, skin side up,
until the skin blackens and bubbles in places. Cover the pepper pieces
with a damp cloth and leave to cool, then peel and slice into strips.

Wash the fish fillets, pat dry, season with salt and pepper and brush
with olive oil. In a saucepan mix the oils and vinegar, season and add the
herbs.

About 20 minutes before you wish to serve the fish, heat the grill.
When hot, cook the fish fillets for 3-5 minutes on each side. Meanwhile,
warm the dressing.

To serve, place the fish on a warmed serving dish, arrange the peppers
and olives around the fillets and spoon over the dressing. Serve with new
potatoes and summer vegetables such as courgettes or runner beans.

Baked fish with herbs Provençale style

This recipe for fish with fresh herbs comes from the Côte d'Azure, from the Hôtel Belair du Cap Ferrat, where in the high season 28 chefs cater for the occupants of 59 rooms.

SERVES 4

115 g (4 oz) fine fresh white breadcrumbs
2 tablespoons each chopped chives, parsley, chervil and basil
sea salt and black pepper
3 tablespoons olive oil
4-8 fillets of plaice, skinned (depending on size)
2 glasses white wine
45 g (1½ oz) butter

Mix the breadcrumbs, herbs, some salt and pepper and 2 tablespoons of oil together. With your fingertips check the fish fillets for any remaining bones and remove them. Place the fillets on a board, skin side up, and divide the crumbs between them. Roll up the fillets and place in a well greased ovenproof dish that takes them in one compact layer.

Drizzle on the remaining oil, season with a little extra salt and pepper and pour half the wine around. Bake in a preheated oven at 190°C/375°F/ Gas 5 for 30 minutes, basting once.

Check the fish is cooked through by inserting the blade of a knife into one fillet. If the fish is tender and opaque it is cooked. Carefully lift the fish on to a heated serving dish and keep warm while you finish the sauce.

Add the remaining wine to the dish and stir, scraping up any bits that have stuck. Transfer the mixture to a saucepan and cook over a high heat to reduce slightly. Beat in the butter to thicken and gloss the sauce, taste and correct seasoning and spoon over the fish. Serve at once with summer vegetables.

BAKED GREY MULLET WITH MINT AND ORANGES

Grey mullet is a fish often rejected for the slightly muddy taste it acquires by living in river estuaries. But well cooked it is delicious. The secret lies in cleaning the fish thoroughly, rubbing off the black skin that lines the stomach cavity with a little coarse salt. I use Seville oranges in this recipe, if I have some in the freezer, but sweet oranges sharpened with lemon juice will do as well.

SERVES 4

1 large grey mullet, 900 g-2.3 kg (2-3 lb)
small bunch of mint
2 small juicy oranges plus 1 lemon, or 3 Seville oranges
30 g (1 oz) butter
sea salt and black pepper

Wash the cleaned fish well, as described above. Pat dry and make 3 deep cuts in each side. Stuff the cuts with mint leaves. Place the fish on a large sheet of well greased foil on a baking sheet and stuff the belly with the remaining mint leaves and slices of lemon or bitter orange. Squeeze the remaining oranges over the fish and season well. Dot with pats of butter.

Fold over the edges of the foil to make a roomy but airtight parcel and bake in a preheated oven at 200°C/400°F/Gas 6 for 20-25 minutes. Serve with new potatoes and peas.

Deep-fried sprats

*I only recently discovered these delicious little fish. They were a great favourite of my
grandmother's, so perhaps I inherited my taste for them from her. They are reasonably
priced and easily eaten, even by the fussiest children. You can eat the bones, or pull
them out, all in one go, from the tail end.*

Serves 4-6

**1 kg (2¼ lb) fresh sprats
4-5 tablespoons plain flour
salt, pepper and chopped parsley or chervil
oil for deep-frying
lemon wedges to serve**

To prepare the fish, take a sharp knife, cut off the tail, then cut away the
vent by making a small nick at either side of it. Turn the fish round and cut
through it, just behind the head, starting from the spine and working
towards the belly. Just before you reach the belly, stop cutting and gently
pull off the head, and the innards will slide out.

Wash the fish under plenty of running cold water and allow to drain.
In a large polythene bag mix the flour with plenty of salt and pepper, and
some herbs. Toss the fish in this mixture, then deep-fry in hot oil until they
are lightly browned, 4-6 minutes. You will probably need to cook the fish
in 2 or 3 batches. Serve at once with lemon wedges.

MARINATED MACKEREL

I learned to love these oily fish when living in Cornwall. They are at their best grilled on a barbecue straight from the sea. If you can't buy mackerel from the quayside, try preparing them this way.

SERVES 4

1 large onion, finely sliced
4-6 medium fresh mackerel
4 bay leaves
2 tablespoons chopped parsley
10 peppercorns
1 teaspoon thyme leaves
1 red chilli, sliced (optional)
1 teaspoon brown sugar
a little salt
⅔ malt vinegar and ⅓ water to cover

Lay half the onion slices in an ovenproof dish large enough to take the fish in one layer. Place the fish on top of the onion, and tuck half a bay leaf in each one.

Scatter the remaining ingredients over the fish and add enough malt vinegar and water to cover.

Cover the dish loosely with foil and bake in a preheated oven at 170°C/325°F/Gas 3 for 40-50 minutes. Leave the fish to cool in the marinade.

Chill, then serve with fresh brown bread and a crisp salad.

Spiced fish and rice cakes

These little fish cakes are based on a traditional Thai recipe. I like the rough texture of the rice and the exotic flavour of the lemon grass and chilli oil. To make ginger juice, squeeze a peeled piece of fresh ginger root in a garlic press.

SERVES 4

225 g (8 oz) fresh haddock, cod, or coley
140 g (5 oz) plain boiled rice
4 spring onions, finely chopped
1 size 2 egg
5 cm (2 inch) piece lemon grass, finely chopped
2 tablespoons finely chopped coriander leaves
½ teaspoon chilli oil
2 teaspoons light soy sauce
½ teaspoon ginger juice
oil for deep-frying

Remove the skin and bone from the raw fish and chop roughly. Place all the ingredients in a food processor. Process in short bursts until finely chopped. Scrape down the sides from time to time and stop processing before the mixture becomes a purée. Put the mixture in the fridge for 1 hour to allow the flavours to develop and blend.

Shape the mixture into small cakes about 5 cm (2 inches) across and fry in hot oil for 3-4 minutes each side or until golden brown. Serve with soy sauce seasoned with a few drops of chilli oil and some stir-fried vegetables.

JUMBO PRAWNS WITH CHILLI SAUCE

Farmed raw jumbo prawns are readily available in most supermarkets. Cooked in this spicy sauce they are good value and make a delicious treat. Put fingerbowls and plenty of paper napkins on the table.

SERVES 2 OR 4

3 tablespoons vegetable oil
2.5 cm (1 inch) cube fresh ginger, peeled and cut into tiny sticks
1 red chilli, sliced
3 spring onions, roughly chopped
2 cloves garlic, crushed and chopped
16 jumbo prawns, thawed
2 tablespoons soy sauce
1 teaspoon chilli oil, or to taste
1 teaspoon sugar
juice of 1 lime or small lemon
1 glass white wine
1 tablespoon butter

Heat the oil in a large frying pan. Put in the ginger and chilli and cook for 60 seconds. Add the onion and garlic and cook for a further minute. Now put in the prawns and cook, turning often, for 3-4 minutes. Add the soy sauce, chilli oil, sugar and lime juice and toss well. Pour in the wine and cook over a high heat until it has evaporated. Add the butter and, as soon as it has melted, serve the prawns with rice or noodles.

PAN-FRIED JUMBO PRAWNS IN GARLIC BUTTER

SERVES 2 OR 4

2 tablespoons oil
115 g (4 oz) butter
16 jumbo prawns (or more)
2-3 plump cloves garlic, crushed and chopped
juice of 1 small lemon
2 tablespoons chopped parsley
sea salt and black pepper

Heat the oil and half the butter in a large heavy bottomed frying pan. Put in the prawns and cook, turning often, for 3-4 minutes. Now put in the garlic and cook for a further minute. Add the remaining butter and the lemon juice. When the butter has melted, add the parsley and season. Stir well and serve at once with crusty bread.

DEEP-FRIED OYSTERS

Cooked oysters are delicious, no matter what the purists say!

SERVES 4

oil for deep-frying
2 dozen plump oysters or large green-lipped mussels
sea salt and black pepper
1 egg, beaten
115 g (4 oz) fresh white breadcrumbs
salad leaves and lemon wedges to serve

Put the oil on to heat and bring a pan of water to the boil. Open the oysters and cook in the water for 30 seconds to firm up. Remove and drain, then dip into the well seasoned beaten egg and roll in the crumbs until well coated. Fry a few at a time for 2-3 minutes until light brown and crisp.

Serve at once on a few small salad leaves with wedges of lemon.

MOULES MARINIÈRE

This is the classic way of cooking mussels: in the manner of the fisherman. An interesting variation is Moules Saintonaigse, in which pungent garlic croûtons are tossed into the dish at the last minute.

SERVES 4

1.3 kg (3 lb) fresh mussels
1 glass dry white wine
1 glass water
2 tablespoons chopped parsley, plus a few stalks
1-2 cloves fresh garlic, crushed and chopped
2 shallots, finely chopped
1 tablespoon butter, kneaded with 1 tablespoon flour
sea salt and black pepper
140 ml (¼ pint) single cream (optional)

Scrub the mussels well under running cold water, pulling off beards and barnacles. Tap mussels that are open and if they don't shut tightly, discard them, along with any broken mussels.

Put the wine and water plus the parsley stalks, garlic and half the shallots in a deep pan and bring to the boil. Tip in the mussels and cook over a high heat, turning often with a long handled spoon. After 3-4 minutes they should all have opened. Any that remain closed after this time should also be discarded.

Remove the mussels from the pan with a slotted spoon, transfer to a serving dish and keep warm while you make the sauce.

Strain the cooking liquor through kitchen paper or muslin into a clean pan, and bring to a rolling boil. Add the remaining shallots and cook for 2 minutes. Beat in the kneaded butter, whisking constantly until the sauce thickens and the flour cooks. Add the chopped parsley and season well, then stir in the cream and heat through.

Pour the sauce over the mussels and serve at once with French bread.

LA MOUCLADE

This rich dish comes from the Charente-Maritime region of France. I love to spend my holidays there, close to the famous oyster and mussel beds of the Gironde estuary. Local seafood combined with spices from merchant ships that called at the ports along the Bordeaux coast inspired this rather eastern recipe.

SERVES 4

2 kg (4 lb) fresh mussels
275 ml (½ pint) water
½ onion, chopped
parsley stalks
a few peppercorns

FOR THE SAUCE
pinch of saffron
140 ml (¼ pint) white wine
½ onion, finely chopped
30 g (1 oz) butter
1 plump clove garlic, finely chopped
1 measure cognac
½ teaspoon mild curry powder
140 ml (¼ pint) double cream
1 tablespoon butter, kneaded with 1 tablespoon flour

Scrub the mussels under running water and remove barnacles and beards. Discard any mussels that are broken or that do not close when tapped. In a large pan heat the water with the onion, parsley stalks and peppercorns until boiling. Put in the mussels and cook over a high heat for 3-4 minutes, turning from time to time until all the shells have opened. Remove from the pot with a slotted spoon and discard any that remain closed. Keep the mussels warm while you make the sauce.

Strain the cooking liquor through muslin. Crush the saffron and soak in the wine. Fry the onion in the butter until it softens, add the garlic and cook for a further minute. Now add the cognac and flame it. Add the wine with the saffron and curry powder, and finally the cream. Bring to the boil and simmer, then add the reserved mussel liquor.

Cook over a high heat until the sauce reduces slightly. Beat in the kneaded butter with a balloon whisk and cook for a further 2-3 minutes to make sure no taste of raw flour remains. Taste and correct seasonings and serve poured over the warm mussels.

For a more elegant presentation, remove all but a dozen mussels from their shells and serve the Mouclade in warm dishes garnished with freshly chopped parsley and the unshelled mussels.

FEUILLETÉ OF MUSSELS WITH TARRAGON

SERVES 4

1 kg (2¼ lb) fresh mussels
onion, peppercorns and parsley stalks for cooking
225 g (8 oz) puff pastry
beaten egg to glaze
1 medium leek, finely sliced
30 g (1 oz) butter
30 g (1 oz) flour
140 ml (¼ pint) single cream
1 tablespoon dry sherry
1 teaspoon tarragon leaves, plus sprigs to decorate
sea salt and black pepper

Scrub the mussels well and cook in water with the seasonings as for Mouclade (page 55). Leave to cool, then remove all the mussels from their shells. Strain the cooking liquor and reserve.

Roll out the pastry and cut 4 rectangles about 5 x 12 cm (2 x 5 inches). Brush thinly with beaten egg. Be careful not to allow the egg to run down the sides of the pastry as it will glue the layers together and prevent the pastry from rising. Bake in a preheated oven at 200°C/400°F/Gas 6 for 15-20 minutes, or until well risen and golden brown. Remove from the oven and allow to cool on a rack until needed.

Cook the leek in a pan of boiling water for 1 minute, drain well and cool in iced water. Melt the butter and add the flour, stirring to form a roux. Add the cream and sherry, beating constantly. Now add the tarragon leaves and enough mussel liquor to give a medium thick sauce. Strain the leeks well and stir in along with the mussels. Cook gently to heat through. Season to taste.

Slice the pastry rectangles to make a sandwich and warm in the oven. To serve, place the pastry base on a plate, spoon on a quarter of the mussels, plus some sauce, and cover with a pastry top. Spoon any remaining sauce around the plate.

Serve at once decorated with sprigs of fresh tarragon.

MEAT &
POULTRY

Summer is the time to enjoy meat dishes that are light and succulent and can be served with the wonderful vegetables and salads that abound.

Successful meat cookery depends on buying the best meat available, which is not necessarily the most expensive, as long as the cut is appropriate to the dish being prepared. This means high quality meat cut from a well hung carcass, properly butchered.

The best piece of advice I can give is to find and use a good local butcher who is prepared to discuss your requirements and to offer the right cut of meat at the right price. You may have to shop around until you find the right one, and it definitely takes courage to ask for, and insist on getting, what you want. But it's worth it – a good relationship with your butcher is a valuable asset to any cook.

Increasingly, people are interested to know how the meat in their local shop has been produced. A butcher who sells free-range chicken knows that not only does the meat taste far better, it goes further, as the flesh is denser in texture.

The second simple rule is that meat should never be overcooked. Unless you are making a stew or casserole, meat should be just undercooked, then rested for 5-10 minutes before serving. The resting period is very important. When meat comes out of the oven or from under the grill, the all-important juices that give it its succulence will be boiling. If you cut the sealed outer layer of the meat at once, the juices will bubble out. Wait for a few minutes and they will stay where they are needed, in the centre of the meat.

Perhaps my favourite summer meat is lamb, and I like to bear in mind the maturing flavour and increasing joint size of fresh meat as the months progress. The earliest lamb has a very delicate flavour and should be treated with great care. I like to cook it simply and serve it with young and tender vegetables. Save the vinegar-based mint sauce for winter and try instead a light hollandaise flavoured with chopped fresh mint. Later in the season you can use the more robust flavours of olive oil, garlic and rosemary along with tomatoes, aubergines and peppers.

Pork sales traditionally fall in the summer, but there are few meats more suited to barbecuing than pork, as it is moderately fatty and happily takes on the rich flavours of barbecue sauces.

I have already made a plea for eating free-range chicken. Game is out of season until September, but if you have a pheasant in the freezer, you can use it in place of chicken in both the escabeche recipe (page 63) and the one for chicken and lentil curry (page 64). A lightly spiced, juicy curry sauce perfectly complements the rich dry meat of the pheasant.

MARINATED CHICKEN BREASTS

This is a recipe for those who like lighter flavours. The chicken breasts are marinated in citrus juice and herbs. Serve them with herb butter (below), a fresh salad and some new potatoes, keeping the flavours simple.

SERVES 4

4 large boneless chicken breasts

FOR THE MARINADE
**grated rind and juice of 1 large orange and 1 lemon
2 tablespoons olive oil
sea salt and black pepper
2 tablespoons chopped herbs**

Wash the chicken and make 3 deep cuts in each piece. Mix the marinade ingredients together and allow the chicken to sit in the marinade in the fridge for at least 1 and up to 4 hours.

Cook the chicken on the barbecue or under a heated grill, for about 20 minutes, turning often and basting with the marinade.

HERB BUTTER

Serve this with the chicken dish above, or with any plainly grilled meat or fish.

**115 g (4oz) soft butter
2 tablespoons chopped parsley
1 clove garlic (optional)
1 tablespoon chopped oregano, basil, tarragon or chervil**

Use a broad bladed knife to chop the herbs into the butter on a board, and mix well. Scrape the mixture together to make a roll. Wrap in greaseproof paper and freeze until needed.

To serve, cut thin slices from the roll of flavoured butter and place on chicken, or other grilled meat, fish, or vegetables.

TANDOORI CHICKEN

This staple of the Indian restaurant can be made quite simply at home and is ideal barbecue food as it tastes better if slightly singed. For a while specialist shops sold miniature tandoors, or Indian clay ovens. My guess is that most of these are now sitting in the garden, planted with geraniums, as they were difficult to use and gave indifferent results.

I use a ready-mixed tandoori paste, such as Patak's, to marinate the chicken. Mixed with yoghurt I find it gives a very good flavour.

SERVES 4

2 kg (4 lb) chicken
juice of 1 lemon
4 tablespoons tandoori paste
140 ml (¼ pint) thick natural yoghurt
oil for basting

TO SERVE
shredded lettuce, onions and lemon wedges

Cut the chicken into 6 pieces and remove all the skin. Cut deep slashes into the joints. Squeeze on the lemon juice and allow the chicken to sit for 30 minutes. Now mix the tandoori paste with the yoghurt and rub it into the chicken. Let this marinate for 2 hours or overnight.

Remove the meat from the marinade and brush with oil. Cook on the barbecue, brushing with oil from time to time and turning often. Cook for about 25 minutes, or until the chicken is cooked through and the edges of the skin start to blacken.

Serve with shredded lettuce and onions, mint and yoghurt chutney (below) and barbecued bread (page 220).

MINT AND YOGHURT CHUTNEY

Serve this with Tandoori chicken (above).

4 tablespoons chopped mint
sea salt and black pepper
½ teaspoon caster sugar (optional)
275 ml (½ pint) thick natural yoghurt
1 teaspoon ground cumin powder

Mix the mint and some salt, pepper and sugar into the yoghurt. Pour into a serving dish and sprinkle the cumin on top.

POACHED CHICKEN WITH TARRAGON VELOUTÉ SAUCE

This is the sort of food that dreams are made of. The bird is gently poached in a flavoured stock, which then forms the base of a velvet-smooth sauce. Choose a free-range chicken for the best flavour and texture. Hens reared in confinement lack flavour and have meat with such little body that it breaks down into shreds long before the dish is ready. French chickens, such as Duc de Bourgogne, are very good, but for choice I pick a Home Farm bird from my local butcher.

SERVES 4-6

1 large free-range chicken (2.5-3 kg/5-6 lb)
salt and black peppercorns
1 large leek
2 carrots
2 ribs celery
bouquet garni of bay leaves, thyme and parsley

FOR THE VELOUTÉ SAUCE
30 g (1 oz) butter
30 g (1 oz) plain flour
600 ml (1 pint) chicken stock
4 tablespoons roughly chopped tarragon
140 ml (¼ pint) cream

Wash the chicken well and season inside and out. Place in a large heavy-bottomed pot and cover with cold water. Cut the leek, carrots and celery into chunks and add them to the pot along with the bouquet garni, a little salt and a few black peppercorns.

Bring to the boil, skimming off any scum that rises to the surface. Simmer the chicken for about 1¼ hours, then insert a skewer into the deepest part of the leg. If the juices run clear, it is cooked.

At least 40 minutes before serving, make the velouté sauce. Melt the butter with the flour in a heavy-bottomed saucepan to make a roux. Add 600 ml (1 pint) cooking liquid from the chicken (or use other stock), and whisk until no lumps remain. Simmer the sauce for 30 minutes over a very low heat, or on a heat diffuser.

About 5 minutes before serving, taste the sauce and reduce a little to improve flavour or consistency if necessary. Stir in the tarragon and cream, reheat and correct the seasoning.

Carve the chicken into serving portions and arrange on a warmed plate. Spoon over a little sauce, handing the rest separately.

POLLO CON AJO

This is a robust Spanish dish: chicken with garlic, white wine and herbs. Use thigh meat, which is sweet and moist and has much more flavour than chicken breast.

SERVES 4

**sea salt and black pepper
8 chicken thighs
4 tablespoons olive oil
3-4 plump cloves garlic, chopped
1 tablespoon chopped herbs
200 ml (⅓ pint) of white wine**

Season the chicken well. Heat the oil in a large pan, and fry the chicken briskly over a high heat until golden. Add the garlic and turn off the heat for a few minutes to allow the oil to cool a little. Now add the herbs and wine and bring the mixture to a simmer. Cover the pan and cook for 15-20 minutes or until the chicken is done. Correct the seasoning and serve hot with rice or crusty bread.

CHICKEN IN ESCABECHE

This recipe for cold chicken comes from Argentina and can be made two days in advance. Escabeche is a vinegar-based sauce that also tastes good with pheasant, partridge and quail.

SERVES 4

**2 kg (4 lb) roasting chicken
3 tablespoons olive oil
1 large carrot, sliced
1 medium sweet onion, sliced
1 small celery heart, sliced
275 ml (½ pint) dry white wine
140 ml (¼ pint) wine vinegar
½ teaspoon thyme leaves
60 g (2 oz) golden sultanas or 115 g (4 oz) green seedless grapes, halved
sea salt and black pepper**

Cut the chicken into small joints and remove all the skin. Heat the oil in a large deep pan and fry the chicken until the joints are sealed and beginning to brown. Add the vegetables and cook, stirring often, for about 5 minutes. Now add all the remaining ingredients except the grapes or sultanas and enough water to cover the chicken. Season well. Simmer for 30 minutes, or until the chicken is tender.

Transfer the chicken and vegetables to a deep serving dish and add the sultanas or grapes. Boil the liquid rapidly to reduce by about half. Pour over the chicken and allow to cool, then refrigerate overnight or longer.

Serve as part of a cold buffet or as a moist and delicious picnic dish.

CHICKEN AND LENTIL CURRY

I love the creamy texture of lentils, and when cooked in the same pot as chicken they absorb so much flavour. This lightly spiced dish makes a good supper for a cooler summer day.

SERVES 4

**2 tablespoons oil
sea salt and black pepper
8 chicken thighs
5 cm (2 inch) piece fresh root ginger, peeled and chopped
1 large onion, chopped
2 plump cloves garlic
2 red chillies
1½ tablespoons each ground cumin and coriander
1 teaspoon turmeric
85 g (3 oz) red lentils
400 g (14 oz) tin chopped tomatoes
lemon juice to taste
about 1 tablespoon sugar
fresh green coriander, chopped**

Heat the oil in a large saucepan. Season the chicken joints well and brown in the hot oil. Remove and reserve. Blend the ginger, onion and garlic to a paste with a little water and put into the pan. Stir-fry this for 2 minutes, then add the chillies and dry spices. Fry the mixture for 2-3 minutes.

Replace the chicken, add the lentils, the tomatoes with their juice and the stock, and bring to the boil. Put on the lid and simmer for about 40 minutes until the chicken is well cooked and the lentils are tender.

If the sauce seems too thin, remove the lid for the last 10 minutes of cooking time to let it reduce.

Stir in lemon juice and sugar to taste, correcting the seasoning with extra salt and pepper as necessary. Garnish with coriander and serve with basmati rice.

Sesame chicken in pitta pockets

The chicken for these pittas can be prepared two days before it's needed. This recipe makes wonderful picnic food or a tasty packed lunch – pack the chicken, bread, salad and dressing separately to be assembled at the last minute.

Serves 4-6

3 chicken breasts, skinned and boned
2-3 tablespoons plain flour
1 size 2 egg, beaten
2-3 tablespoons sesame seeds
oil for frying
shredded iceberg lettuce
finely sliced red peppers
bean sprouts
shredded spring onions

For the marinade
1 tablespoon light vegetable oil
1 tablespoon dark soy sauce
½ teaspoon sesame oil

For the dressing
2 tablespoons light vegetable oil
1 tablespoon sherry or wine vinegar
1 teaspoon light soy sauce
1 teaspoon clear honey
½ teaspoon sesame oil

Mix the marinade ingredients together. Cut the breasts into strips and marinate them for 30 minutes.

Dip each breast into the flour, then coat with egg and roll in the sesame seeds. Shallow-fry in hot oil for about 15 minutes, until golden and cooked through. Drain on kitchen paper and allow to cool, then store in the fridge until needed.

Mix the dressing ingredients together and serve the chicken in salad-filled pitta pockets drizzled with dressing.

SOUTHERN-FRIED CHICKEN

*The first time I tasted home-fried chicken I realized what all the fuss was about. My
hostess came from the Deep South and prided herself on her family recipes. This
chicken is as close as I can come to Tricia's secret coating.*

SERVES 4

8 chicken pieces: thighs, breasts or drumsticks
140 ml (¼ pint) single cream or creamy milk
1 teaspoon each celery seasoning, garlic salt and paprika
½ teaspoon ground black pepper
about 85 g (3 oz) self-raising flour
oil for deep-frying

FOR THE CREAM GRAVY
about 1 tablespoon seasoned flour
about 415 ml (¾ pint) milk

Wash the chicken pieces and pat dry with kitchen paper. Marinate them in
the cream or milk for about 15 minutes. Mix the seasonings into the flour.

Lift the chicken pieces from the cream and allow any excess to drain
off. Now roll them in the flour, making sure they are thoroughly coated.
Heat 5-7.5 cm (2-3 inches) oil in a deep pan until it will brown a cube of
bread in 60 seconds. Fry the chicken in a single layer over a medium heat,
turning often until it is cooked through and golden brown all over. Test the
chicken by pricking the deepest part with a skewer. If the juices run clear,
it is done.

To make the cream gravy, pour off most of the hot oil from the pan
leaving any residue and pan scrapings. Return the pan to the heat and stir
in the flour (you can use leftover seasoned flour from the coating), to give
a blond roux.

Add the milk, mixing well to make sure the sauce is smooth. Simmer
for 4-5 minutes, until it looks rich and glossy. Taste and correct the
seasoning.

Serve the hot chicken with cream gravy and mashed potatoes.

CHICKEN FAJITAS

Serve these fajitas with guacamole (page 68) and chilli tomato salsa (page 68). If you can't find flour tortillas in your supermarket or delicatessen, use white pitta bread or chapatis.

SERVES 4

675 g (1½ lb) chicken breasts, boned and skinned
1 tablespoon cumin seeds
2 dried red chillies
½ teaspoon salt
6 black peppercorns
1 tablespoon oregano leaves
1 large clove garlic
2 tablespoons oil
2 tablespoons lime juice
1 large mild Spanish onion, sliced

TO SERVE
warm flour tortillas
soured cream
guacamole (page 68)
tomato salsa (page 68)

Cut the chicken into strips and place in a shallow dish. Crush the dry spices using a pestle and mortar, crush the cumin, chillies, salt and pepper, then add the oregano and garlic, and work with the oil and lime juice to a thick paste. Rub this into the chicken pieces and leave to marinate for 1 hour.

Heat a large heavy frying pan or griddle and brush lightly with oil. Cook the chicken, turning often, until slightly charred and cooked through. Remove and cook the onions with a little more oil.

To assemble the fajitas, first spread them with soured cream, pile on chicken and onion, and roll them up. Serve at once with guacamole and tomato chilli salsa.

GUACAMOLE

Guacamole should always have a rough texture, so don't make this in a blender or food processor. Make this dip at the last moment if possible to preserve its wonderful colour.

---

2 ripe avocados
lemon juice to taste
1 small mild onion, chopped
1 large ripe tomato, peeled, seeded and chopped
sea salt and black pepper
a few drops Tabasco

Mash the avocado flesh with a fork, adding about 1 tablespoon lemon juice. Mash in the onion and tomato, season with salt, pepper and Tabasco and add extra lemon to taste. Guacamole may be stored in a covered bowl in the fridge, but it will gradually lose its colour.

FRESH TOMATO AND CHILLI SALSA

Be careful not to touch your eyes when handling chillies, as the oil can cause painful smarting.

---

450 g (1 lb) ripe tomatoes, peeled, seeded and chopped
1-2 small green chillies, seeded and chopped
1 small mild onion, finely chopped
2 tablespoons chopped fresh coriander leaves
1 tablespoon fresh lemon or lime juice
sea salt and black pepper

Mix all the ingredients together, and season to taste with salt and pepper. Leave for at least 1 hour before serving to allow the flavour to mature.

BREAST OF DUCK WITH GREEN GOOSEBERRY SAUCE

Make this delicious recipe with the duck breast and save the legs for confit (page 70).

SERVES 4

4 boneless duck breasts with skin on
sea salt and black pepper
oil for frying the bread
4 slices white bread

FOR THE SAUCE
450 g (1 lb) gooseberries
175 ml (6 fl oz) duck or chicken stock
2 tablespoons white wine vinegar
1 teaspoon mild mustard
3-4 blades of mace
30 g (1 oz) butter
a little sugar

Start by making the sauce. Top and tail the gooseberries and place in a saucepan with all the other sauce ingredients, except the butter and sugar, and cook until you have a thick purée. You may sieve the sauce at this stage to remove the skins, but it's not strictly necessary. Beat in the butter and add only enough sugar to mellow the sauce; it should not taste sweet.

Season the meat well and cut several gashes through the skin of each breast. Heat a heavy frying pan and cook the breasts, skin side down, without adding fat or oil. Fry for about 5 minutes, and cook the other side. Fat will run from the gashes in the skin. The duck should be crisp on the skin side and pink in the centre. Remove and keep warm.

Add a little oil to the pan and quickly fry the bread. Serve each duck breast on a croûte with the gooseberry sauce, some new potatoes and summer vegetables.

Confit de canard with green lentils

This recipe was given to me by Gary Rhodes, chef at London's Greenhouse Restaurant. Green lentils make a perfect accompaniment for crisply cooked confit or you can serve it on a bed of green leaves with vinaigrette dresssing. Use the breast meat from the duck to make the recipe with green gooseberry sauce (page 69). If you can buy extra duck legs, do so, as this recipe is easily expanded.

Note that for best results, confit should be stored for several weeks before it is used.

SERVES 4

1 duck
450-900 g (1-2 lb) lard
clear honey (optional)

FOR THE MARINADE
1 shallot, finely chopped
1 clove garlic, crushed
about 1 teaspoon each thyme and crumbled bay leaves
2 tablespoons sea salt
1 teaspoon crushed peppercorns
¼ teaspoon each powdered cloves and allspice

FOR THE GREEN LENTILS
225 g (8 oz) green lentils
2 tablespoons duck fat
2 shallots, chopped
1 clove garlic, crushed and chopped
1 teaspoon thyme leaves
600 ml (1 pint) duck or chicken stock
1 glass white wine
2-3 tablespoons juice from cooking duck (optional)
sea salt and black pepper

Cut off the breasts and reserve (see introduction). Cut off the leg joints and trim excess skin. Put the carcass, neck and skin into a roasting pan and roast in a medium oven at 180°C/360°F/Gas 4 for 2-3 hours, until all the fat has been rendered. Pour off the fat and store in a cool place. You can now discard the bones or boil them with seasoning vegetables to make a duck stock.

Mix the marinade ingredients together and rub them well into the duck legs. Leave to marinate in the fridge overnight.

Shake off any excess marinade and pat the legs dry. Melt the rendered duck fat in a large pan. Put the pieces of duck into the melted fat and add sufficient extra melted lard to raise the level of the fat above the duck. Simmer over a very low heat for 2 hours, or until it is very tender.

Remove the duck legs to a sterilized jar or glass bowl and pour on enough fat to cover. Allow the remaining fat to cool, then remove it from the underlying juices and store separately for later use. Even though this is not pure duck fat it is well seasoned and very good for roast potatoes. The juices can be frozen until needed for the green lentils.

Store the confit in the fridge for at least 2 weeks and up to 3 months before using.

Wash the lentils well and allow to drain. Melt the fat and fry the shallot and garlic until soft. Now put in the thyme and the lentils and cook, stirring from time to time, for about 2 minutes. Add the stock, wine and duck juice and season with pepper. Simmer for 35-40 minutes until the lentils are soft. If there is still a lot of liquid, boil for a few minutes to reduce the sauce. Season with salt to taste.

Meanwhile, prepare the confit. Remove the legs from the fat, scraping off as much as possible. Preheat the oven to 200°C/400°F/Gas 6. Brush the duck with honey, if you like. Cook the duck for 10-15 minutes until crisp.

Serve on a bed of green lentils.

Duck and bulgur salad

It is worth cooking a duck especially to serve cold in this wonderful salad.

Serves 6

1 medium duck
sea salt and black pepper
285 g (10 oz) bulgur
600 ml (1 pint) warm water
2 thin skinned oranges plus 1 tablespoon orange juice
2 tablespoons raisins
3 tablespoons olive oil
1 medium red onion, finely chopped
2 plump cloves garlic, finely chopped
6 tablespoons chopped parsley
2 tablespoons chopped mint
squeeze of lemon juice

Wash the duck well and season inside and out. Cook on a rack over a roasting pan in a preheated oven at 200°C/400°F/Gas 6, for about 80-90 minutes or until the juices run clear when a skewer is inserted into the deepest part of the leg. Allow to cool, then remove all the meat from the carcass and chop into bite-sized pieces.

Meanwhile, put the bulgur to soak in the water for 45 minutes. Grate the zest from one orange and reserve. Discard the peel, pith and pips from both oranges, then chop the flesh. Soak the raisins in the tablespoon of orange juice.

Drain the bulgur, squeeze out any excess water and place in a large bowl. Add the oil and toss well. Now add all the remaining ingredients, and the duck, and toss again. Taste and adjust the seasoning. Leave for about 30 minutes to allow the flavours to blend, then toss once more and turn on to a serving dish.

This looks very pretty garnished with fresh herbs and edible flowers.

LAMB ROASTED WITH SUMMER VEGETABLES

SERVES 4

2 medium kohlrabi, peeled and finely sliced
1 medium aubergine, sliced
2 small heads fennel, sliced
2-3 fat cloves garlic
4 spring onions, chopped
sea salt and black pepper
1 kg (2¼ lb) knuckle or leg of lamb
6 small ripe tomatoes, quartered
140 ml (¼ pint) water
4 tablespoons olive oil
1 tablespoon chopped mixed herbs

Place the kohlrabi, aubergine and fennel in a large ovenproof dish and add the garlic and the spring onions. Season the meat well and place on the vegetables. Dot the tomato pieces around the dish and pour on the water. Drizzle over the oil and sprinkle on the herbs.

Cook in the oven, preheated to 200°C/400°F/Gas 6, for 1½ hours, or until the lamb is pink in the centre and the vegetables are done. Baste the meat about twice during cooking time.

Carve the lamb into thick slices and serve with the vegetables and some olive oil roasted potatoes.

LAMB BOULANGER

This is a glorious way to cook new season's lamb, and dates from the time when the village women, who had no ovens of their own, would use the baker's shop to cook the Sunday joint. Long slow cooking allows you the morning free to spend in the garden.

SERVES 6-8

**8 medium potatoes, peeled and sliced
3 tablespoons olive oil
1 large onion, finely sliced
2 cloves garlic, crushed and finely chopped
1 tablespoon chopped rosemary or tarragon
2.5 kg (5 lb) shoulder of lamb
sea salt and black pepper
1 litre (1½ pints) light vegetable stock**

Put the potato slices into a large bowl of cold water and wash off the starch, then drain. Brush a large ovenproof dish with about 1 tablespoon of the oil, put in the potatoes, onions, garlic and herbs and mix together well. Roughly flatten the vegetables and place the lamb, skin side down, on top. Season well and drizzle on the remaining oil. Pour the stock around the meat and place the dish in a preheated oven, at190°C/375°F/ Gas 5.

After 1 hour, turn the meat the right way up and baste the vegetables. Roast for a further hour, by which time the meat should be golden brown, the potatoes cooked through and most of the stock absorbed. Remove the meat to a warm place to rest for 15-20 minutes. Turn up the heat, replace the dish in the oven and allow the potatoes to crisp.

Carve the meat in the normal manner and serve with the stock-enriched potatoes and green beans or lightly cooked spinach.

ROAST SHOULDER OF LAMB WITH DAMSON SAUCE

I have always loved the shoulder joint of lamb. It is by far the sweetest meat and, if carefully cooked, need not be fatty. In this recipe early damsons are made into a sharp rosemary-infused sauce that perfectly counterpoints the rich meat.

SERVES 4-6

**2 tablespoons olive oil
1 clove garlic, crushed
leaves from 1 sprig rosemary
sea salt and black pepper
well trimmed shoulder of lamb**

FOR THE SAUCE
**225 g (8 oz) damsons
4 tablespoons red wine
1 shallot, finely chopped
1 clove garlic, crushed
2-3 sprigs rosemary**

Season the oil with garlic, rosemary, salt and pepper and brush all over the meat. Roast in a preheated oven at 200°C/400°F/Gas 6 for 20 minutes per 450 g (1 lb), turning the joint over twice to ensure it is a rich golden brown all over.

Meanwhile, for the sauce, simmer the damsons in the wine with the shallot, garlic and rosemary until the fruit is very soft. Rub the sauce through a sieve, pressing hard to extract as much flavour as possible. Pour into a clean pan.

Once the meat is cooked, transfer it to a warmed dish and allow to rest for 10 minutes. Pour off most of the fat from the pan, then whisk the pan juices into the hot plum purée. Continue whisking over a medium heat until the sauce thickens, then taste and correct the seasoning. You may, if you like, add a little honey or sugar at this stage.

Serve the lamb garnished with fresh rosemary and hand the sauce separately.

Roast rack of herb-encrusted lamb

Ask your butcher to remove the backbones from the racks of lamb to make the carving easier, as well as almost all of the fat, as this will not cook under the crust.

SERVES 4-6

2 x 6-chop racks of lamb
4 slices wholemeal bread
small bunch each mint, chives and parsley
1-2 cloves garlic
sea salt and black pepper
2-3 tablespoons olive oil

Put the bread, herbs and garlic into a blender and process until everything is finely chopped. Add seasoning and the oil, process briefly, then press half the mixture on to the skin side of each lamb rack.

Lay the racks in a roasting dish, crust uppermost, and cook in a pre-heated oven at 220°C/425°/Gas 7 for 20 minutes if you like your lamb rare, 30 minutes if you like it medium, and 40 minutes if you prefer it well done.

Serve with new potatoes, peas and redcurrant jelly.

Ham in parsley aspic with quails eggs

Jambon persille is one of my favourite French holiday foods. This special version has quails eggs set in clear jelly sitting on top of the ham and parsley. It makes a delightful Easter lunch dish.

Clarifying the stock is a little tricky and not strictly necessary, but it will give a wonderfully glossy jelly.

SERVES 6

2 kg (4 lb) gammon or hock joint
6 quails eggs
celery, carrot and leek for poaching
bouquet garni
bay leaves
peppercorns
2 sachets gelatine powder
4 tablespoons dry white wine
scant tablespoon white wine vinegar
2 egg whites, plus shells
very large bunch fresh parsley, chopped

Soak the ham in water overnight to remove some salt.

Boil the quails eggs in water for 3-4 minutes, drain and cool quickly in iced water.

Put the ham and seasoning vegetables into a large saucepan with the bouquet garni, bay leaves and peppercorns, and cover with cold water. Bring to the boil and skim off the scum. Allow the pot to simmer with the lid ajar for about 2 hours until the meat is very tender.

Allow the ham to cool in the liquor, then remove any skin and most of the fat. Cover and chill. Cut the ham into cubes for the next stage in the recipe.

Meanwhile, strain the liquor into a clean jug and chill until the fat has set, then carefully remove and discard the fat.

Sprinkle the gelatine over the wine and allow to swell then transfer it with the vinegar and 1 litre (1½ pints) cooking liquor to a deep saucepan. Crush the egg shells and whisk with the egg whites until frothy. Pour this mixture into the pan of stock and, whisking continuously, bring the stock to the boil. As soon as the stock starts to rise up the pan, stop whisking and turn off the heat. Once the mixture subsides turn the heat on again. Don't whisk, just let the mixture boil and rise up the sides of the pan. Repeat once more. The object of this is to trap the impurities in the egg white crust. Don't worry if the crust breaks a little – just be as careful as you can.

Scald a teatowel and lie it over a deep bowl. Carefully slip the crust on to the cloth and gently pour the stock through both the crust and the cloth to finally strain it. By now the aspic should be quite clear.

Shell the quails eggs and arrange them in the base of a medium soufflé dish. Pour over enough aspic to cover, and allow to set. Arrange the cubed ham over the set jellied eggs. Mix the parsley into the remaining aspic and spoon over enough to cover the ham. The jelly should be beginning to thicken as you do this. Chill until needed.

To serve, dip the dish into very hot water for 30 seconds. Wipe dry, then invert on to a beautiful plate.

Glazed meat terrine

This splendid dish makes a perfect centrepiece for a buffet or summer lunch. Make sure it doesn't sit in the sun or the beautiful jelly will melt.

Serves 10-12

450 g (1 lb) veal (trimmed offcuts)
170 g (6 oz) streaky bacon, rinded
675 g (1½ lb) boned and skinned belly of pork
2 plump cloves garlic
6 juniper berries
½ teaspoon black peppercorns
seeds from 2-3 cardamom pods
thyme
sea salt and black pepper
2 tablespoons brandy
2 chicken breasts, boned and skinned
4 tablespoons white wine
1 tablespoon olive oil
grated nutmeg
170 g (6 oz) ham
2 tablespoons shelled pistachio nuts

To finish
115 g (4 oz) ready-to-eat prunes
275 ml (½ pint) white wine
115 g (4 oz) ready-to-eat apricot halves
275 ml (½ pint) apple juice
1 sachet gelatine

Mince the veal, bacon and pork twice, using the coarse blade of the mincer. Put the garlic, juniper berries, peppercorns, cardamom seeds, thyme and a teaspoon of coarse salt into a mortar and crush with a pestle to make a paste. Alternatively grind the spices electrically and add to the crushed garlic. Knead the mixture into the meat along with the brandy, making sure everything is well mixed. Cover and refrigerate for 2 hours.

Meanwhile, slice the chicken breasts into fine strips. Mix the wine and oil with some pepper and a pinch of nutmeg, and marinate the chicken in this until needed. Slice the ham into strips the same size as the chicken strips.

Press half the pork mixture into the base of a 7.5 x 23 cm (3 x 9 inch) springform tin, then arrange the chicken, ham and pistachios on top. Press on the remaining pork mixture. Place the terrine in a roasting dish with 2.5 cm (1 inch) boiling water. Bake in a preheated oven at 150°C/300°F/ Gas 2 for about 1½ hours. The terrine is cooked when it has shrunk from the sides of the tin and the juices run clear when the centre is pierced with a skewer. Allow to cool, then refrigerate overnight.

To finish, put the prunes in the wine, and the apricots in the apple juice, and allow both to soak overnight.

The next day, remove the fruit and arrange on top of the terrine. Pour the soaking liquids together into a jug and make up to 600 ml (1 pint) with hot water. Sprinkle the gelatine over about 3 tablespoons of this liquid, and warm it until the granules dissolve. Add the measured liquid and cool until it is on the point of setting. Carefully pour the jelly over the terrine, spooning extra over the fruit to make sure it is well glazed. Refrigerate until completely set, then unclip the ring mould and serve.

FRIED CALVES LIVER WITH BALSAMIC VINEGAR

Balsamic vinegar is an expensive delicacy from Modena in Italy, a soft sweet wine vinegar that has been matured for many years in wooden casks. Its unusual flavour can be appreciated to good effect in this fashionable recipe.

SERVES 4

2 tablespoons olive oil
4 x 115-140 g (4-5 oz) calves liver
115 g (4 oz) pancetta or streaky bacon, finely chopped
2 shallots, finely chopped
2 tablespoons balsamic vinegar
275 ml (½ pint) light chicken stock
sea salt and black pepper

Heat the oil in a large frying pan and fry the liver over a high heat, turning only once, until crisp on the outside but still rare in the centre. Remove and keep warm.

Add the pancetta and the shallots and cook rapidly, stirring until they are golden brown. Deglaze the pan with the balsamic vinegar, scraping up all the bits that have stuck, and add the stock. Boil rapidly to reduce by half.

Correct the seasoning, return the liver to the pan for 30 seconds, then serve at once with potatoes mashed with olive oil.

PORK STEAKS WITH FRESH PEACHES AND GINGER

The ground ginger and almonds in this recipe are used in a traditional English manner to thicken and enrich the sauce.

SERVES 4-6

2 tablespoons light olive oil
1 large onion, finely chopped
4-6 lean pork steaks
2 teaspoons ground ginger
2 medium carrots, finely diced
60 g (2 oz) ground almonds
sea salt and black pepper
275 ml (½ pint) chicken stock
4 medium peaches
1 tablespoon clear honey, warmed

Heat the oil in a large heavy pan and gently fry the onion until pale gold. Now add the pork steaks, two at a time, and fry until lightly coloured on both sides.

Remove the meat from the pan and put in the ginger, carrots and almonds. Season and stir well. Add the stock, replace the meat and bring to a simmer. Cover the pan and cook for 30-40 minutes, or until the pork is tender.

Meanwhile, place the peaches in a deep bowl, cover with boiling water for 2-3 minutes, then slip off the skins. Slice the fruit neatly, discarding the stones.

Once the meat is cooked, take the chops from the sauce and lay them in an overproof dish. Arrange the peach slices on top of the steaks and brush with the honey. Cook under a preheated grill for 3-4 minutes, until the peaches are hot and the honey starts to caramelize.

Meanwhile, pour the contents of the pan into a liquidizer and process until smooth. Return to a clean pan and reheat. Taste and correct the seasoning, and simmer the sauce to thicken if necessary. Spoon the sauce around the pork steaks and serve with rice or mashed potatoes.

PASTA, RICE & POLENTA

These versatile staple foods are quick to cook, economical, and good for you. They often form the basis for vegetarian meals, and combine equally deliciously with simple sauces of meat or fish. The recipes here are mostly Italian in inspiration, though I have added others from Spain, Portugal and India.

It is possible today to buy fresh pasta from most supermarkets and specialist shops, but much of it is made by mechanical extrusion. Rolled pasta is a much superior product, but also more costly. I like to make my own pasta having found out how simple it is to do. The revelation was like a conversion and I at once became a born-again fresh pasta maker. As with making bread, it does take time and effort, but the process is therapeutic and the results are incomparable. Use a strong, high-gluten flour as you would for bread-making, fresh eggs and fine salt. Some recipes call for olive oil and these make supple pasta suitable for stuffing.

When not using homemade pasta I prefer to use a good quality dried egg pasta. There is a wide range of such pastas on the market and Italian delicatessens make a good hunting ground. I had always scoffed at those fearfully expensive handmade pastas, such as Cipriani, but having tried them I have to admit that they taste ambrosial. I always allow about 115 g (4 oz) dried pasta or 175 g (6 oz) fresh pasta for a main course serving, with 85 g (3 oz) dried and 115 g (4 oz) fresh for a first course portion. Of course you can vary this according to preference, taking into account what will be served alongside the pasta.

Once you have drained the cooked pasta, drizzle on a little oil and tip into a warmed serving dish. Using two forks, lift the pasta gently to separate the noodles and to spread the oil through them. Always serve pasta into warmed dishes.

I always keep a lump of parmesan cheese in the fridge: double-wrapped in foil, it stores well. I like to grate it on to pasta or risotto, or shave curls or flakes from the block.

Buy your parmesan from a shop with a good turnover, preferably an Italian delicatessen, and taste before you part with your money. If you have only ever eaten ready grated parmesan from a cardboard tube you are in for a revelation with the first bite.

Parmesan also makes a delicious addition to a cheeseboard, its grainy texture and salty flavour perfectly balancing fruit such as grapes or figs.

A good risotto has a creamy texture and a wonderful depth of flavour. These qualities come from the Italian rice arborio, which has a soft starchy coating and a firm centre. The rice becomes sticky as it's cooked, and constant stirring ensures that it forms its own sauce deeply impregnated with your chosen flavouring ingredients. The flavour can come from something as simple as a little good chicken stock or a bunch of fresh garden herbs. Beat in butter and parmesan cheese just before serving and you'll have a marvellously unctuous risotto. Spooned into bowls and served with bread and salad, it's a meal fit for kings.

Finally in this chapter, we come to polenta, which can be served like risotto, or shaped into a cake and allowed to set, whereupon it can be grilled or fried.

BASIC PASTA DOUGH

SERVES 4-6

300 g (10 oz) strong white bread flour
3 size 2 eggs
¼ teaspoon fine table salt

Mix the ingredients together and knead until you have a smooth glossy dough, adding a little extra flour if the dough sticks to your hands or the board. Leave to rest for 15 minutes, then divide into 3 or 4 pieces.

Roll through a hand-operated machine set at ever decreasing thicknesses until the correct thickness is reached.

The rolled dough can be used at once in recipes for stuffed pasta, or allowed to dry for a few minutes, then cut into noodles.

Bring plenty of salted water to the boil in a large saucepan. Add the pasta and return to the boil. Cook for 2-3 minutes from this point, until the pasta is al dente, or shows a slight resistance when you bite it. Drain in a large colander. Put a knob of butter or a tablespoon of olive oil into the hot empty saucepan and return the noodles to it, tossing them well.

WHOLEMEAL PASTA

SERVES 4-6

140 g (5 oz) wholemeal flour
140 g (5 oz) strong white flour
3 size 2 eggs
¼ teaspoon fine table salt

Make the pasta as for basic pasta dough (above).

HERB PASTA

SERVES 4-6

a good handful fresh soft herbs: chervil, tarragon, basil, marjoram or dill
¼ teaspoon fine table salt
2 tablespoons olive oil
2 size 2 eggs
250 g (9 oz) strong white bread flour
1-2 tablespoons water

Place the herbs, salt, oil and eggs in a food processor and chop finely. Now add the flour and sufficient water to give a stiff dough.

Turn out the dough and knead for about 5 minutes until smooth. Rest for 5 minutes, then proceed as for basic pasta dough (page 84).

RICH SAFFRON PASTA

SERVES 4-6

2 tablespoons water
2 tablespoons olive oil
1 sachet saffron powder
2 size 2 eggs, plus 1 extra yolk
250 g (9 oz) strong white flour
generous pinch of salt

Warm the water and oil together and sprinkle on the saffron powder. Let this stand for 5 minutes to allow the maximum colour infusion.

Beat the eggs with the yolk, add to the saffron mix, then add this to the flour and salt. Knead well to form a smooth dough, rest for 5 minutes and proceed as for basic pasta dough (page 84).

Black pasta

Exotic looking black pasta gets its colour from squid ink, which means it goes wonderfully well with fish sauces. You can extract the ink yourself from fresh squid, but it's easier to order little sachets of ink from fishmongers or fine food shops.

Serves 4-6

285 g (10 oz) strong white bread flour
2 size 2 eggs
2 tablespoons olive oil
2 tablespoons water
1 teaspoon salt
2 sachets squid ink

Make the dough as for basic pasta dough (page 84), kneading well to get an even colour. Roll out to the penultimate mark on the pasta machine, then allow the strips of dough to dry for 15 minutes. Cut them into very fine angel hair noodles. They will take only 2-3 minutes to cook.

Tomato pasta

It can be difficult to get enough colour into this pasta, as the texture is weakened by the ratio of too much tomato paste to flour. However, a delicate pink will suffice, and makes a pretty dish served alongside black, yellow or green noodles.

Serves 3-4

200 g (7 oz) strong white flour
1 teaspoon salt
1 size 2 egg
1 tablespoon olive oil
2 tablespoons tomato purée

Make the pasta as for basic pasta dough (page 84).

PARSLEY AND PARMESAN PESTO

One of the most successful pasta sauces has to be pesto, classically a combination of pine nuts, hard cheese, olive oil and masses of fresh basil. This wonderfully rich and fragrant sauce comes from the rocky mountainous coastal area of Liguria.

In Ancient Rome a type of pesto was made from bitter herbs and goats cheese, and the earliest recorded recipe is said to date from the time of Virgil. The word 'pesto' means 'pounded', so there is no need to feel too constrained about what you put into pesto.

SERVES 4

**60 g (2 oz) freshly grated parmesan
2 tablespoons pine kernels
2-3 cloves juicy garlic
1 large bunch flat-leaf or English parsley
sea salt and black pepper
140 ml (¼ pint) virgin olive oil**

Put all the ingredients except the oil in a blender and process until everything is thoroughly ground together. Add the oil through the feed tube with the motor running. Start with a very fine stream, as if you were making mayonnaise. The finished sauce should be about the consistency of thick cream.

Spoon into a dish and leave for 15 minutes to allow the flavours to develop. Stir into hot pasta.

CHEDDAR, FROMAGE FRAIS AND PARSLEY SAUCE

This is a similar sauce to pesto, but a little lighter.

SERVES 4

**115 g (4 oz) fromage frais
115 g (4 oz) mature Cheddar cheese
large bunch of parsley
2 cloves fresh garlic
black pepper to taste
1½ tablespoons olive oil**

Blend all the ingredients together in a food processor until fairly smooth and thick. Stir into hot pasta.

VEAL AND ROSEMARY SAUCE

SERVES 4

2 tablespoons olive oil
1 medium onion, finely chopped
1 plump clove fresh garlic, chopped
450 g (1 lb) minced veal
600 ml (1 pint) passata (Italian sieved tomatoes)
sprig of fresh rosemary, plus chopped rosemary
sea salt and black pepper

Heat the oil in a saucepan and sauté the onion until lightly browned. Add the garlic and cook for a few moments, then add the veal. Stir until lightly coloured, then pour in the passata and add the sprig of rosemary, seasoning well.

Simmer for 20-25 minutes, then remove the rosemary sprig. Add the chopped rosemary, correct the seasoning, and stir into hot pasta.

FRESH TOMATO SAUCE

725 g (1½ lb) ripe tomatoes
1 shallot, chopped
1 plump clove garlic
1 tablespoon olive oil
Salt and pepper
1 teaspoon chopped fresh chives

Fry the shallot and garlic in the oil in a large saucepan.

Roughly chop the tomatoes and put into the pan, season with a little salt and pepper and bring to the boil. Cover the pan and simmer for 30 minutes.

Sieve the sauce and return to the pan. Simmer uncovered, until the sauce is the desired thickness. Check the seasoning and stir in the chives.

HAM-FILLED RAVIOLI WITH FRESH SAGE AND CREAM SAUCE

Choose a dry salty ham for these ravioli. The idea for the sauce comes from my good friend, restaurateur Antonio Carluccio, whose wonderful Italian food shop in Neal Street, London, inspires and delights me.

SERVES 4

1 quantity fresh pasta dough (page 84)
170 g (6 oz) full flavoured ham, finely minced
3-4 tablespoons double cream

FOR THE SAUCE
140 ml (¼ pint) each double and single cream
45 g (1½ oz) freshly grated parmesan
1 tablespoon chopped fresh sage
sea salt and black pepper

Roll out the dough as described on page 84, keeping the sheets covered with film until needed.

Mix the ham with the double cream to give a stiffish paste, and season with pepper.

Place small spoonfuls of the ham mixture at intervals on the dough and brush between them with a little water. Carefully lay another sheet of dough over the top and press between each mound to seal the ravioli. Cut between the ravioli, then lay them on a film-covered tray until needed. Continue until all the filling is used. Don't worry if the ravioli look a little uneven: that is part of the charm of homemade pasta.

Bring a large pan of water to the boil and cook the ravioli for 3-4 minutes. Drain well and pour in the cream, cheese and sage, and season lightly with salt and pepper. Toss gently to mix, then turn into a warmed dish and serve at once.

SPINACH AND RICOTTA-FILLED RAVIOLI

This is a wonderfully fresh tasting ravioli. I have given instructions for large individual pasta envelopes lined with spinach leaves, which look wonderful but do take a little time to make. If you are rushed for time, simply put all the spinach in the filling. This will make 6 ravioli. Serve 1 as a starter or 2 as a main course.

SERVES 3-6

1 batch rich saffron pasta dough (page 85)
225 g (8 oz) fresh baby spinach leaves
225 g (8 oz) ricotta
1 size 2 egg
60 g (2 oz) freshly grated parmesan
sea salt and black pepper

Roll out the dough as described on page 84, keeping the sheets closely covered with film until needed.

Wash and dry the spinach. Remove half the leaves, choosing the largest, and blanch these in a pan of boiling water for 1 minute. Drain and refresh with cold water then lay the leaves on a clean teatowel to dry.

Put all the remaining ingredients in a food processor and blend well.

On a sheet of film, arrange enough blanched spinach leaves to form a 15 cm (6 inch) square. Place a large tablespoon of filling in the centre of this square, then gather up the film to enclose the filling in the spinach leaves. Remove the film. Place the spinach wrapped parcel on a sheet of pasta and top with another sheet. Press the dough together around the filling, then trim the edges to give an even finish. Keep the finished ravioli covered with film while you work, and continue until all the filling is used. Cut any unused dough into noodles and dry for future use.

Cook the ravioli in plenty of boiling salted water for 2-3 minutes, then drain and serve with a little olive oil, cream or fresh tomato sauce.

EGG-FILLED RAVIOLI

These large individual ravioli look spectacular – when cut open the soft yolk runs out
to form the sauce. This will make 6 ravioli. Serve 1 as a starter or 2 as a main course.

SERVES 6

1 batch fresh pasta dough (page84)
225 g (8 oz) ricotta
60 g (2 oz) freshly grated parmesan
1 bunch watercress, coarse stalks removed
sea salt and black pepper
6 size 3 eggs
olive oil
chopped herbs to garnish

Roll out the dough as described on page 84. Cut out 12 x 10 cm (4 inch)
squares, and cover closely with film. Cut the remaining dough into noodles
and dry for future use.

Process the cheeses and watercress in a blender, season well, and
spoon into a piping bag with a wide nozzle. Take a pasta square and pipe
on a circle of cheese filling, leaving a 5 mm (¼ inch) margin and a hollow
in the centre. Carefully break an egg into the hollow. Lightly dampen the
edges of the pasta and cover with a second square, pressing down well to
seal. Continue until you have made 6 ravioli. Handle them very gently.

Fill a deep frying pan with water and bring to the boil. Simmer the
ravioli for 3-4 minutes, remove carefully with a slotted spoon and serve
drizzled with a little olive oil and sprinkled with herbs.

LASAGNE WITH SUMMER VEGETABLES

Leaves of fresh pasta are layered with summer vegetables and bathed in a light tomato and herb sauce. This simple dish is assembled just before serving and is much lighter than a meat lasagne.

SERVES 4

1 batch fresh herb pasta (page 85)
2 medium aubergines
salt and black pepper
olive oil for frying
2 medium red onions, sliced
3 medium courgettes, sliced
fresh tomato sauce (see page 88)
30 g (1 oz) parmesan, flaked
basil leaves

Roll out the pasta as described on page 84, and cut into 12 x 15 cm (6 inch) sheets. Keep covered with film. Cut any remaining pasta into noodles and dry for future use.

Slice the aubergines 5mm (½ inch) thick and sprinkle with salt. Allow them to sweat for 30 minutes, then rinse and pat dry. Season with pepper, then fry in hot oil until brown on both sides. Remove and keep hot. Fry the onion until wilted and lightly coloured. Remove and keep hot.

Bring a large pan of water to the boil and simmer the pasta sheets for 2-3 minutes, then drain.

Blanch the courgettes in boiling water for 2 minutes. Drain and keep warm. Heat the tomato sauce.

Arrange a sheet of pasta on each of 4 warmed plates and divide the aubergine slices between them. Top with a further sheet of pasta and the onions. Finish with the last sheet of pasta and the courgettes. Spoon over some hot tomato sauce and garnish with parmesan and fresh basil to serve.

FRESH PASTA WITH SALMON IN A CREAM AND LEMON SAUCE

This is an elegant and delicate summer dish.

SERVES 4

1 large lemon
bay leaf
peppercorns and salt
1 shallot, peeled
450 g (1 lb) salmon (boned, skinned weight)
450 g (1 lb) fresh pasta noodles (see page 84)
275 ml (½ pint) double cream
1 tablespoon chopped chervil, tarragon or parsley

Scrub the lemon under hot water to remove any wax, then finely grate the zest. Squeeze out the juice. Put the lemon shells into a large saucepan with the bay leaf, peppercorns, a pinch of salt and the shallot. Add the salmon. Bring to the boil and gently poach the fish for 4-5 minutes. Take off the heat. Leave in the water while you make the sauce.

Bring a large pan of water to the boil and cook the pasta for 2-3 minutes until al dente.

Meanwhile, pour the cream, lemon juice and zest into a nonstick pan and bring to the boil. Simmer to thicken and reduce. Flake the salmon and fold gently into the cream.

Drain the pasta and place in a heated serving dish. Pour over the salmon and sauce and scatter on the chopped herbs. Serve at once.

TAGLIATELLE WITH CHICKEN AND MUSHROOMS

SERVES 4

2 chicken breasts, skinned and boned
3 tablespoons olive oil
1 small onion, sliced
1 clove garlic, chopped
170 g (6 oz) button mushrooms, sliced
1 glass sherry or white wine
fresh tarragon, chopped
1 batch fresh pasta noodles (page 84)
115 g (4 oz) crème fraîche
sea salt and black pepper

Cut the chicken into strips and reserve.

Heat the oil in a frying pan and cook the onion until it wilts and colours. Add the garlic and fry for a few moments. Put in the chicken and fry, stirring often until the strips brown, then add the mushroms and stir-fry for 2-3 minutes.

Deglaze the pan with the sherry, add the tarragon and boil rapidly until most of the liquid evaporates. Meanwhile, cook the pasta until al dente. Drain.

Stir the crème fraîche into the sauce and heat through. Season to taste and serve on the hot noodles.

TAGLIATELLE WITH ANCHOVIES AND SUN-DRIED TOMATOES

The sauce is quickly made by pounding the ingredients together – no cooking needed.

SERVES 4

8 sun-dried tomato halves
1 teaspoon capers
340 g (12 oz) dried tagliatelle
1 small can anchovies in oil
1-2 cloves garlic, crushed
zest and juice of ½ lemon
6 tablespoons olive oil
4 tablespoons freshly chopped mixed chives and parsley

If the sun-dried tomatoes are not in oil, soak them in hot water for 5 minutes to allow them to soften. Slice them into fine strips. If you use salted capers, wash them well first.

Bring a large pan of salted water to the boil and cook the noodles according to the instructions on the packet. Drain and return to the pan.

While the pasta cooks prepare the sauce: place the anchovies, garlic, capers and lemon zest in a mortar and crush to a paste with the pestle, adding the lemon juice when the ingredients start to break down. Now add the oil a little at a time until you have a roughly homogeneous sauce.

Toss the sauce into the hot noodles, and add extra salt, pepper or lemon juice to taste. Tip the pasta into a warmed serving dish and pile the herbs on top. Top this with the tomato strips and serve at once, tossing everything together at the table.

FUSILI WITH SPRING VEGETABLES

This spiral pasta dish is made unusual by the addition of lots of chopped herbs and some grated lemon zest.

SERVES 4

340 g (12 oz) dried fusili
115 g (4 oz) tiny carrots
115 g (4 oz) baby corncobs
115 g (4 oz) asparagus tips
115 g (4 oz) mangetout peas
115 g (4 oz) baby courgettes
4 tablespoons olive oil
grated zest of 1 lemon, plus 1 tablespoon lemon juice
2 tablespoons each chopped fresh chervil and chives
sea salt and black pepper
freshly grated parmesan

Bring 2 large pans of water to the boil. Cook the pasta in the first pan according to the instructions on the packet.

Cut the vegetables into 2.5 cm (1 inch) pieces, leaving the carrots whole. Cook the vegetables in the second pan, starting with the carrots, followed by the corncobs, then the asparagus, followed by the mangetout peas, and finally the courgettes. If you leave a gap of about 1 minute between each different vegetable they should all be cooked at the same time.

Two minutes after adding the courgettes, drain the vegetables and mix with the hot pasta. Toss in the olive oil, lemon zest and juice and the herbs, and season with plenty of salt and pepper. Serve at once with parmesan.

Spaghetti marinara in a paper bag

*When you open the greaseproof envelope at the table, the wonderful aroma of shellfish
and herbs is released. The spaghetti must be slightly undercooked when it is put into
the bag, and the sauce a little thinner than usual.*

*If you can't find greaseproof paper 45 cm (18 inches) wide, use turkey size
aluminium foil.*

Serves 2-3

225 g (8 oz) dry spaghetti
3 tablespoons butter
1 small bulb fennel, finely sliced
1 medium onion, finely chopped
1 tablespoon plain flour
140 ml (¼ pint) fish stock, or mussel cooking liquor
140 ml (¼ pint) white wine
140 ml (¼ pint) single cream
sea salt and black pepper
1 tablespoon freshly chopped chervil, dill or tarragon,
either: 900 g (2 lb) mussels, steamed and shelled, plus 115 g (4 oz) frozen
prawns; or: 400 g (14 oz) tin shelled vongole (clams) in brine, drained

Melt the butter in a saucepan and cook the fennel and onion until wilted.
Sprinkle on the flour, then stir in the stock, wine and cream to make a
thinnish white sauce. Do not use the brine from the tinned clams as the
finished dish will be too salty. Simmer for 2-3 minutes. Season with a little
salt and pepper and stir in the herbs.

Cook the spaghetti in a large pot of boiling water for 5 minutes, then
drain.

Have ready 2 x 45 cm (18 inch) squares of greased foil or paper. Place
one on a large baking sheet and tip the spaghetti into the centre of it, then
pile the mussels and prawns or clams on top. Pour over the sauce, and top
with the remaining sheet of paper or foil. Fold the edges together firmly to
give a steamproof seam. If using greaseproof paper, brush the outside
lightly with oil.

Cook the bag in a preheated oven at 180°C/360°F/Gas 4 for 10
minutes. Serve at once.

Basic risotto

This simple risotto is delicious served with a spoonful of pesto (page 87), roasted red peppers or sautéed vegetables.

Serves 4-6

about 1.2 litres (2 pints) good chicken or vegetable stock
60 g (2 oz) butter
2 tablespoons olive oil
2 shallots, finely chopped
300 g (10 oz) arborio rice
4 tablespoons white wine
60 g (2 oz) freshly grated parmesan

Put the stock to simmer.

Melt half the butter and the oil in a large heavy-bottomed pan and cook the shallots until transparent. Add the rice and cook, stirring, until it is well coated.

Now add the wine and turn up the heat. When the wine has evaporated, start adding the stock, a ladleful at a time, stirring constantly. Allow the rice to absorb the liquid fully before adding more stock. Keep adding the stock and stirring the risotto for about 15 minutes, until the sauce is creamy and the rice is al dente, neither too tender, nor too firm.

Beat in the cheese and the remaining butter, cover the pan with a folded teatowel and the lid and leave to sit, off the heat, for 5 minutes, then serve.

RISOTTO OF COURGETTES AND COURGETTE FLOWERS

I love the aroma of this risotto and its increasingly creamy texture as it cooks. It does take about 20 minutes and must be made just prior to eating, but sip a glass of fruity wine while you stir, and the problems of the day seem to slip away.

SERVES 4-6

1.2 litres (2 pints) good vegetable or chicken stock
60 g (2 oz) butter
2 tablespoons olive oil
1 medium onion, finely chopped
450 g (1 lb) small green courgettes, diced
310 g (11 oz) arborio rice
sea salt and black pepper
6 tablespoons white wine
4-6 courgette flowers
60 g (2 oz) freshly grated parmesan

Put the stock on to heat.

Melt half the butter plus all the oil in a heavy bottomed saucepan and sauté the onion until it is transparent and very soft. Add the courgettes and cook for 2-3 minutes. Now put in the rice and a little seasoning and stir until everything is coated with butter. Turn up the heat and add the wine, cook until it has evaporated, then start adding the stock a ladleful at a time, stirring constantly.

After about 15 minutes test the rice. It should be al dente – both creamy and toothsome. Roughly chop or tear the courgette flowers and stir them in with the remaining butter and the cheese.

Cover the pan with a cloth and the lid and leave for 5 minutes, then serve.

RADICCHIO RISOTTO

In Tuscany, where radicchio grows like a weed, it is often cooked and served either as a hot vegetable or in a wonderfully purple pink risotto.

Follow the recipe above, substituting 2-3 heads of radicchio. Shred them and add in place of the courgettes and courgette flowers. This recipe serves 4-6 people.

PANCETTA AND MUSHROOM RISOTTO

If you collect wild mushrooms, you can make even a few stretch to a meal for four people with this risotto. The smoky flavour of the bacon complements perfectly the richness of the mushrooms. I have made this recipe with Slippery Jack, Bay Boletus and puffballs, and all were delicious. (Never take risks with wild mushrooms you don't recognize, and always consult a guide.)

SERVES 4-6

about 1.2 litres (2 pints) chicken stock
2 tablespoons olive oil
115 g (4 oz) pancetta or smoked streaky bacon, rinded and chopped
2 medium shallots, finely chopped
115-225 g (4-8 oz) mushrooms, chopped
340 g (12 oz) arborio rice
1 glass white wine
sea salt and black pepper
30 g (1 oz) butter
60 g (2 oz) freshly grated parmesan

Put the stock on to heat.

Put the oil in a large pan and cook the pancetta or bacon until the fat runs, then add the shallots and cook until transparent. Add the mushrooms and cook for 3-4 minutes until they wilt. Next add the rice and cook, stirring, for 2 minutes, until it is well coated with butter.

Add the wine, turn up the heat, and cook until it has evaporated. Start adding the stock a little at a time, stirring constantly, and only adding more stock when the rice has absorbed all the liquid. Continue to cook, adding stock, until the rice is bite-tender and the sauce creamy.

Taste and correct the seasoning, then beat in the butter and parmesan cheese. Cover the pot with a folded cloth and the pan lid and leave to rest for 5 minutes, then serve.

MIXED SEAFOOD RISOTTO

This is another wonderful summer risotto. If you are holidaying on the coast you can often find a few mussels or cockles among the rocks, and perhaps cast a line into the sea for flat fish. Otherwise you can buy a little of whatever takes your fancy at your local fish merchant.

SERVES 4-6

450 g (1 lb) mussels, cockles or clams
225 g (8 oz) prepared weight white fish or young squid
sea salt and black pepper
60 g (2 oz) butter
2 tablespoons olive oil
2 shallots, chopped
300 g (10 oz) arborio rice
1 small glass white wine
1.2 litres (2 pints) mild fish stock
60 g (2 oz) freshly grated parmesan
225 g (8 oz) shrimps or prawns

Scrub the mussels, cockles or clams under plenty of cold running water and remove any mussel beards. Heat a little water in a large pan and cook the prepared molluscs for a few minutes over a high heat until the shells open. Discard any that remain closed.

Remove all the molluscs from the pan with a slotted spoon and keep warm in a covered bowl in the oven. Strain the cooking liquor into a bowl and reserve.

Cut the fish into chunks or cubes, season lightly and reserve.

Now melt half the butter in a heavy pan, add the oil and cook the shallots until transparent. Add the rice and cook, stirring, until it is coated in butter, then pour on the wine. Cook until this evaporates, then add the mussel cooking liquor.

When the liquor has been absorbed, start adding the stock a ladleful at a time, only adding the next ladleful when all the liquid has been absorbed. Test the rice and when it is bite-tender, add the parmesan. Mix well and cover with a folded teatowel and a lid while you finish the fish.

Heat the remaining butter in a separate pan and quickly fry the fish or squid until cooked through. Add the shrimps or prawns and toss until heated. Tip the fish, seafood and mussels into the risotto, toss gently with two forks and serve at once.

SUMMER VEGETABLE PILAF

A pilaf is simpler to cook than risotto, and this one is flavoured with saffron and served with chopped herbs and cream.

SERVES 4-6

1 sachet saffron powder
2-3 tablespoons white wine or water
4 tablespoons light vegetable oil
1 medium onion, finely chopped
1 clove garlic, crushed and chopped
300 g (10 oz) easy-cook or American long-grain rice
generous 600 ml (1 pint) vegetable stock
sea salt and black pepper
115 g (4oz) tiny carrots
115 g (4 oz) shelled peas
115 g (4 oz) red pepper, sliced
115 g (4 oz) green beans, sliced
140 ml (¼ pint) single cream
1 tablespoon each chopped tarragon and parsley

Put the saffron powder to soak in the wine or water.

Heat the oil in a deep pan and fry the onion until lightly browned. Add the garlic and cook for 1 minute. Now put in the rice and toss well in the oil. Pour in the saffron mixture and the stock and season lightly. Bring to the boil, cover and simmer for about 12 minutes. Add the vegetables and cook for a further 5-8 minutes, or until the rice is tender and the liquid absorbed. It may be necessary to add a little extra stock.

Taste the rice and correct the seasoning. Turn the pilaf on to a warmed serving dish, toss lightly to mix everything together and pour over the cream. Sprinkle on the herbs and serve at once.

SPICED CHICKEN PILAF

This hearty pilaf makes a good buffet meal or one-pot supper.

SERVES 4

4 chicken breasts, boned and skinned
3 tablespoons oil
1 medium onion, chopped
2 carrots, diced
10 cm (4 inch) stick cinnamon
6 cardamom pods, crushed
sea salt and black pepper
60 g (2 oz) raisins
60 g (2 oz) slivered almonds
310 g (11 oz) basmati rice
60 g (2 oz) shelled garden peas
2-3 tablespoons chopped green coriander

FOR THE MARINADE

275 ml (½ pint) thick natural yoghurt
2 teaspoons ground cumin
2 teaspoons ground coriander
1 teaspoon turmeric
3 cardamom pods, crushed
½ teaspoon ground black pepper
¼ teaspoon cayenne pepper, or to taste
2.5 cm (1 inch) piece fresh ginger root, peeled and finely grated
2 plump cloves garlic, crushed

Cut the chicken breasts into cubes. Mix the marinade ingredients together and rub into the chicken. Leave for 1-2 hours.

Heat the oil in a heavy casserole and fry the onions until golden brown. Add the carrots, spices, salt, pepper, raisins and almonds and fry for a further 2-3 minutes, until the almonds colour.

Now add the chicken and toss to coat, scraping up any bits that stick to the bottom of the pan. Continue to cook for 2-3 minutes, then add the rice and stir well. Add about 600 ml (1 pint) water, stir once more, then bring to the boil. Cover with a lid and simmer over a low heat for 15-20 minutes, checking from time to time and adding a little more water if necessary, until the rice is bite-tender and the chicken cooked through.

Taste and correct the seasoning, then add the peas and toss into the rice mixture. Cover the pan with a folded cloth and the lid and leave off the heat for 5 minutes.

Turn out on to a warmed serving dish, tossing with two forks to fluff up the rice. Scatter on the coriander and serve.

Aurora's Father's seafood paella valencia

I remember well my first taste of paella in a café on the coast north of Barcelona. A blackened, oil-encrusted dish appeared from the open-air kitchen and we feasted on mussels, chicken and rice. Only one of our party tried the squid, and I'm ashamed to say it wasn't me.

Recently a Spanish friend, Aurora, showed me how to make this dish. Aurora's father, in common with many Spanish men who in the normal course of events never cook, makes a magnificent paella. Traditionally eaten for Sunday lunch, paella can be made with any combination of chicken, pork, spicy sausage, seafood and vegetables. The best part of the dish is said to be the pegado or golden crust that sticks to the paella pan; it is from this large two-handled cooking dish – the paellera – that paella gets its name.

Paella is wonderful cooked outside over a barbecue and can be tended while you talk and enjoy the sunshine.

SERVES 4-6

450 g (1 lb) mussels
about 1 litre (1½ pints) stock
1 pinch saffron or 1 sachet saffron powder
3 tablespoons olive oil
1 medium onion, chopped
2 cloves garlic, chopped
1 red pepper, seeded and chopped
2 large tomatoes, peeled, seeded and chopped
about 225 g (8 oz) cleaned squid
2 small chicken breasts, boned and skinned
about 225 g (8 oz) boned and skinned white fish
285 g (10 oz) paella or risotto rice
60 g (2 oz) tiny peas

TO FINISH
cooked prawns
quartered hardboiled eggs
strips of roasted red peppers

Scrub the mussels and remove the beards. Put a little water into a large pan and bring to the boil. Put the mussels in all at once and cook, stirring often, over a high heat until the shells open. Remove the pan from the heat, take the mussels from the pan with a slotted spoon and reserve. Strain the pan juices through muslin or kitchen paper into the stock.

Toast the saffron in a long handled spoon over a gas flame until it begins to give off a rich aroma. Crush between two spoons, mix this into about half a cup of the stock and leave to soak.

Heat the oil in a paellera or a very large deep frying pan (a wok won't do). Cook the onion, garlic and red pepper until they soften, then add the tomato, and cook for a few minutes. Cut the squid, chicken and fish into smallish pieces, add them to the pan and stir into the hot oil until they become translucent.

Add the rice and stir, cooking gently for 2-3 minutes. Add the saffron and two-thirds of the stock and simmer for 10 minutes. Add the peas and the mussels, and continue to cook, adding extra stock as necessary until the rice is tender but still has a bite to it. Remove some of the mussel shells if you wish.

Arrange the prawns, eggs and roasted pepper strips on the cooked dish, then cover with foil. Leave to rest for 5 minutes, then serve with a green salad and a bowl of garlic mayonnaise (page 134).

PORTUGUESE CHICKEN AND RICE

This is a very easy recipe and one that has proved popular with children. For more sophisticated palates I sometimes add artichoke hearts about 5 minutes before the dish is ready to serve.

SERVES 4

3 tablespoons olive oil
8 chicken thigh joints
1 large onion, chopped
1 red pepper, seeded and sliced
2 fat cloves garlic, crushed
115 g (4 oz) kabanos or other spicy sausage, chopped
225 g (8 oz) long-grain rice
400 g (14 oz) tin chopped Italian tomatoes in juice
scant 600 ml (1 pint) chicken stock
sea salt and black pepper
Tabasco (optional)

Put the oil into a heavy saucepan or deep frying pan with a lid, and fry the chicken pieces, a few at a time, until golden all over. Don't rush, as browning the chicken well makes a real difference to the flavour of the finished dish.

Remove the chicken from the pan, and fry the onion and pepper until wilted. Add the garlic and fry for a further minute. Now put in the sausage and the rice and stir-fry for about 2 minutes.

Return the chicken to the pan and add the tomatoes and stock. Season with salt, pepper and Tabasco, and bring to the boil. Simmer over a low heat for 25-30 minutes, until the rice is cooked and no pink juices run when a skewer is inserted into the chicken. If there is still some liquid in the pan turn up the heat to evaporate, taking care not to burn the rice.

Turn the mixture out on to a heated serving dish and scrape out the delicious crust that has formed. Serve at once.

CATALAN BLACK RICE

Often served 'wet', i.e. with some stock left unabsorbed, arroz negro or black rice is cooked in a caldero, a deep, flat bottomed dish, and coloured with squid ink. Most recipes I have found in books use only seafood, but I have also eaten it with chunks of chicken and rabbit.

Squid ink can be bought in tiny plastic sachets from fish shops or delicatessens. It keeps well and may also be used in risottos and black pasta.

This recipe makes a good party meal.

SERVES 6-8

4 medium squid
6 tablespoons olive oil
6 chicken thighs, skinned, boned and diced
1 medium onion, finely chopped
2 cloves garlic, finely chopped
1.2 litres (2 pints) chicken or fish stock
450 g (1 lb) Spanish or risotto rice
4 sachets squid ink or ink sacs from squid
340 g (12 oz) raw prawns, peeled if liked
sea salt and black pepper
chopped parsley and lemon quarters to serve

Have the fishmonger clean and skin the squid for you. Cut them into 5 cm (2 inch) pieces. Heat the oil in a large heavy frying pan or casserole dish about 30 cm (12 inches) across and 5 cm (2 inches) deep. Fry the squid and chicken until browned, then remove. Now fry the onion and garlic until browned and add about three quarters of the stock. Bring to the boil, then add the rice. Put back the chicken and squid and simmer for 10 minutes.

Stir the squid ink into the remaining stock and add to the rice along with the prawns. Stir gently to ensure the ink colours the rice evenly and continue to cook until all the stock has been absorbed and the rice is bite-tender. If the rice is not cooked by the time the stock has been absorbed, add a little water.

When the rice is ready, taste and correct the seasoning, then leave to sit for 5 minutes, off the heat. Scatter on the chopped parsley and serve with lemon wedges.

POLENTA

Polenta is a staple of northern Italy. Made from ground corn, it can be served as a meal in itself, like rice, with cheese crumbled into it – blue cheese is wonderful – or with a robust chilli tomato sauce, or you can leave it to set into a cake, then cut it into slices to grill or fry. Plain, grilled or fried, it makes an excellent accompaniment for stews, casseroles, grilled meat and fish.

Buy instant polenta, as you need to stir it for only 5-10 minutes, as opposed to 45 minutes for the traditional variety.

SERVES 4

**1 litre (1½ pints) water
sea salt and black pepper
225 g (8 oz) instant polenta
60 g (2 oz) butter
60 g (2 oz) freshly grated parmesan**

Bring the water plus a little salt to the boil in a deep saucepan and, when it is bubbling vigorously, pour in the polenta in a thin stream. Stir constantly with a wooden spoon to prevent any lumps forming.

Lower the heat and, still stirring, cook until the mixture forms a thick mass and begins to come away from the sides of the pan. Beat in the butter and the cheese and season to taste.

You can serve the polenta at once or pour it into a loaf tin and allow to set.

To fry polenta, simply cut slices from the loaf and cook in hot oil until golden brown. To grill polenta, cut slices from the loaf, brush with seasoned olive oil and cook under a preheated grill until browned. Thick slices of polenta can also be cooked on a barbecue grill.

SALADS
&
DRESSINGS

Almost any vegetables, seeds, fruits and nuts can be included in salads. Tender leaves and shoots, grated roots, beans, berries and stone fruit marry wonderfully in oil and vinegar dressings to give unusual flavour combinations.

Nevertheless, my favourite remains a simple salad of mixed green leaves. In France, where it is known as mesclun, young tender salad leaves are mixed with herbs such as chervil and rocket, then dressed with oil and vinegar. You can buy a mesclun from some seed merchants. Planted in something as small as a grow-bag, it can be cut as needed, leaving the roots to grow on and provide more leaves to vary your salad bowl.

Here are some tips for making good salads.

• Plunge salad leaves into a deep bowl of cold water and whoosh them around. Always lift the leaves from the water leaving the grit to sink to the bottom, rather than draining the water from the bowl. Spin the leaves dry in a salad spinner or by simply gathering them into a teatowel, grasping the corners together firmly, and shaking out the water. This is best done out of doors.

• Always tear the leaves to the size you want rather than cutting them, as the cut edge will brown quickly.

• Store the leaves in a polythene bag or a bowl covered with film in a cool dark place until needed. Don't let delicate leaves come into contact with the freezing unit in the fridge.

• Rubbing the inside of a wooden salad bowl with garlic and seasoning the bowl with oil improves both the taste of the salad and the look of the bowl, but it's much more important to have a big bowl than a wooden one. Salad leaves are fragile and must not be crushed. The bowl should be big enough to enable you to toss, not stir, the salad, so that each leaf is well coated with dressing.

• All salad ingredients should be of excellent quality.

• Fragile ingredients like avocado, which quickly goes brown unless brushed with lemon juice, or colourful ones like beetroot, which can

turn everything else purple, should be added at the very last moment.
• Choose edible flowers that are small, or break them down into individual petals.
• Some onions can be deliciously sweet and juicy and so perfect for salads, while others have a coarse peppery flavour that needs cooking. Red onions are often recommended for salads because of their attractive appearance. However, do taste before you serve them, as not all red onions have a delicate flavour.
• Scallions or spring onions can also be peppery with the white part more robustly flavoured than the green. Finely chopped, the green ends of spring onions make a good garnish for soups or casseroles.
• The dressing should balance the choice of salad. Delicate leaves need only the lightest dressing. When you include more robust flavours such as bulb fennel or chicory you can use a robust oil sush as extra virgin Tuscan oil with its wonderful peppery bite. Only when dressing iceberg or other crisp but flavourless lettuces should you use one of the ebullient transatlantic dressings like Thousand Island or blue cheese.
• Always add the dressing to delicate leaf salads at the time of serving. Mix the ingredients together in a screw-topped jar and taste to make sure you have the balance of flavours you enjoy. When you are ready to eat the salad, give the jar a good shake and pour the dressing over the leaves. Toss them gently but thoroughly with your hands or long-handled salad servers.
• Robust salads, such as those containing pasta, fruit and chunky vegetables, are best dressed ahead to allow the flavours to marry.
• When it comes to making salad dressings, there are many different oils and vinegars to choose from. See the section below for advice on olive oils, nut oils, vinegar and dressings.

Oils

Olive oil, combining as it does a wonderful flavour and a low level of saturated fats, has experienced an extraordinary boom in sales as talk of the 'healthy' Mediterranean diet and the popularity of Italian food grows. But as with all things some olive oils are wonderful and others not so good.

You must first decide what type of oil you are looking for. Oils from various producing countries all have individual characteristics, in much the same way that wine from different vineyards does not taste the same. Even within a country (such as Italy) oils fom different areas will taste remarkably different. The Northern Tuscan oils have a very definite hot peppery kick but the Calabrian oils from the warm south are smoother and sweeter. Generally speaking the more yellow the oil, the more oily it will taste. The lush yellow oils from Spain are wonderfully mellow and rich on the palate; the greener French oils from Provence are still oily but have more fragrance and the bright green Italian oils are the strongest in flavour and the least oily tasting.

Acidity plays a great part in an oil's quality, the rule being the lower the acidity the better the oil. The more processing the olives have had the higher the acidity, hence the price and popularity of the first cold pressing extra virgin oil.

In times gone by the olives were hand gathered before being ground to a pulp with huge stone rollers. The extraction of the oil is much the same today. The pulp is layered between mats which are then piled into a mechanical press. The first pressing oil is then allowed to settle before being filtered and bottled and then sold at a a premium price. The leftover olive paste is then heated to encourage it to release more oil. This may still be labelled 'virgin' oil but the label will not contain the magic words 'cold first pressing extra virgin'. After this process chemicals are added to the pulp and the last of the oil removed. This oil is then refined and blended and is sold as olive oil with no fancy prefix. This is the oil you can buy in large bottles for cooking. The importance of reading oil labels cannot be over-stressed as much oil is produced in North Africa, Greece and Turkey, transported to Italy or France and simply bottled there. While there is nothing wrong with these oils, it is important to know where the oil was actually produced.

Olive oils, unlike vintage wines, do not improve with age; they keep well for about a year stored in a cool dark place. I like to cook with olive oil and use a blended oil for this purpose. Chips are delicious fried in olive oil. The general rule is never to cook with an extra virgin oil (the whole point of such oils being that they have never been heated), but I do love eggs, fried crisp at the edges, in a rich extra virgin oil and slipped onto a slice of toasted, country-style bread.

One final word. I find that recipes from different countries are best cooked in their own country's oils, so, for instance, when making paella I use a Spanish oil and when making rouille I use French.

Nut oils

The most readily available of these are both French: walnut oil from the central, Dordogne region and hazelnut oil from the South West.

No one travelling in the Dordogne could be unaware of walnuts. Walnut trees line every roadside, and the nuts crunch under your tyres as you drive. Street shops and markets are called noix and walnuts appear in almost every conceivable guise. There are walnut breads, cakes and tarts, walnut candies, ice creams and liqueurs. Walnuts are served with meat and fish and, picked when still green, are steeped in red wine and made into a robust celebration drink. They are also ground and pressed for their oil which is used extensively in this area as a salad dressing. As this oil does not keep well buy a small amount, store in the fridge and use quickly.

Hazel trees abound in the area of France around Agen, home of the wonderful pruneaux. While many regional recipes combine both crops in desserts and candies, hazelnut is increasingly available for use as a salad dressing.

Groundnut oil
This used to be known as peanut oil and is a clean-flavoured, light-bodied oil that is particularly suitable for use in oriental cooking. When I make a salad that uses soy sauce or ground peanuts this oil provides the perfect base.

Flavoured Oils
Flavoured oils can easily be made at home. Don't use a strong flavoured base oil; groundnut or a blended olive oil are ideal, and use plenty of your flavouring ingredient. Remember that all ingredients must be absolutely clean and any herbs used should be picked in the morning when full of flavour and then allowed to dry completely on kitchen paper before being placed in the oil. A jar of oil containing a sterilised, empty lobster claw has a wonderful aroma of lobster and would make an exellent base for dressing a seafood salad for example. I make chilli oil by adding crushed dried red chillies to oil and leaving them to steep for about 2-3 months.

Vinegar
I have often thought that it would be possible to tell which country you were visiting simply by trying its local vinegar. So often this seems to mirror the favourite drink of the nation. In England malt vinegar comes hand in hand with beer brewing; in Scotland distilled vinegar is favoured; in China the staple vinegar is made from rice wine, Northern France has cider vinegar and Spain has sherry vinegar.

Vinegar is formed when acetifying bacteria react with alcohol and its blending process. Malt vinegar is matured for about four months but balsamic vinegar can be aged for up to one hundred years!

Balsamic Vinegar

Balsamic, meaning smooth or soft, vinegar is made in Modena, Italy from the Trebbiano grape. Must, which is cooked grape skins, is added after the first maturation and helps give the vinegar its attractive sweetness. The vinegar is stored in small wooden casks, softening and concentrating as it ages. It is truly in a class of its own and should be used more as a rare seasoning than as a vinegar. A few drops added to a sauce lift and enhance the flavour. It makes a delicious dressing for salad, or when used to deglaze the pan after frying meats such as duck breast or calves liver. It helps cut the fatty taste and gives a wonderful depth of flavour to all kinds of dishes. My daughters like a few drops sprinkled on strawberries and it makes a dramatic difference to some ice cream recipes.

Wine Vinegars

Red, white and even champagne vinegars are very easily obtainable today. Wine vinegar has a sharp but delicate flavour that I find most suitable for general use. I prefer to use a white wine vinegar for most light-coloured dishes but don't worry if you only have red.

Rice Vinegars

Red, black and distilled rice vinegars are mainly used in Chinese or Thai cooking. The darker vinegars have very strong flavours and colours.

Sherry Vinegar

A light, dry, full flavoured vinegar from Spain, sherry vinegar marries well with oily fish.

Flavoured Vinegars

Fruit vinegars are delightful to look at and taste wonderful. Packed into pretty bottles and clearly labelled, flavoured vinegars make delightful gifts. I make them very simply by adding about 175 g (6 oz) of soft fruit, such as raspberries or blackcurrants, to a bottle of white wine vinegar, leaving it to mature for about a month. Herb-flavoured vinegars are as simple to make. As with flavoured oils, clean and dry herbs are steeped in the chosen vinegar, again for about a month. Tarragon, rosemary and thyme give particularly pleasing results and I also like to make spiced vinegars using peeled ginger root, chillies and whole, peeled cloves of garlic.

Malt and Distilled Vinegars

I have left these until last as the flavour of a good matured malt vinegar is far too strong for most cooking and I find distilled vinegar a little weak. These vinegars come into their own when making pickles or chutneys. The robust flavour of malt vinegar is especially good in heady, spiced mixtures based on recipes for chutneys and relishes from the Indian empire. Distilled vinegars are best used if you want to keep the colour of the pickle clear, so pickled pears, peaches and piccalilli should all be made with it.

French Dressing

True French dressings use French olive oil with its light oily taste, wine vinegar, some Dijon mustard and a little garlic. The proportions are usually one part vinegar to three parts oil, the other ingredients being added according to personal taste, seasoning with salt and freshly ground black pepper. As I like a slightly sweet dressing I often add a little caster sugar to this mixture, or better still, a small spoon of clear honey. Chopped fresh herbs are another optional ingredient. Choose your herbs to complement the flavours in the main dish.

The French also love to use nut oils. Keep dressings made from these oils simple: a mixture of lemon juice and walnut or hazelnut oil seasoned with salt and pepper. There is no need to use mustard or sugar. Use this dressing on a salad of green leaves garnished with a few chopped nuts of the same variety as the oil.

Italian Dressing

This has almost no parallel with commercially-made dressings that are sold under this name. To me a good Italian dressing is made using extra virgin Italian oil and either lemon juice for a sharp dressing or balsamic vinegar for a soft one. The quantities depend on individual taste with the vinegar or lemon juice acting as just discernible background tastes. It is, after all, the oil that is the main ingredient and, having possibly paid a small fortune for a good oil, you would be foolish to disguise the taste with unnecessary ingredients.

TOMATO SALAD

Well made, a tomato salad is a dish fit for kings, so choose firm, ripe, fragrant tomatoes and serve them at room temperature. When buying tomatoes from the supermarket, choose under-ripe ones and keep them in a bowl in the kitchen, using them as they are ready. I never store tomatoes in the fridge, as the cold masks their delicate flavour.

Basil leaves should always be torn and not sliced, as they bruise easily and lose their beautiful bright green colour.

SERVES 4

450 g (1 lb) firm ripe tomatoes
sea salt and black pepper
extra virgin olive oil
fresh basil leaves

Slice the tomatoes and arrange them in a single, overlapping layer on a serving plate. Season lightly with salt and pepper and drizzle over some oil. The acidity in the tomatoes makes vinegar unnecessary. Scatter over some basil leaves and leave for about 15 minutes before serving.

SALADE TRICOLORE

Choose creamy ripe avocados, large full-flavoured tomatoes and, if possible, buy mozzarella made in Italy from buffalo milk.

SERVES 4-6

4 large tomatoes
2 mozzarella cheeses
2 ripe avocados
extra virgin olive oil
a few drops balsamic or wine vinegar
fresh basil leaves

Slice the tomatoes and the mozzarella. Peel the avocado, remove the stone and slice the flesh. Arrange the slices alternately on one large or 4 or 6 small plates and drizzle with oil and vinegar. Top with basil leaves and serve at once with fresh bread.

ROASTED FENNEL AND RED PEPPER SALAD

The fennel and red pepper develop a beautifully sweet flavour as they cook. The garlic is an optional but delicious extra.

SERVES 6

**2-3 red peppers, seeded and sliced into 4
4-5 heads fresh fennel, trimmed
sea salt and black pepper
4-5 tablespoons olive oil
1 bulb fresh garlic
about 1 teaspoon fresh thyme leaves**

Preheat the grill. Lay the peppers on the grill pan, skin side uppermost and cook until the skin bubbles and blackens. Remove from the heat and cover the peppers with a damp cloth. When cool, peel off the skins and slice into fine strips.

Meanwhile, slice the fennel about 5mm (¼ inch) thick. Season the oil and brush it on to the fennel slices. Separate the cloves of garlic and place them, unpeeled, in an ovenproof dish with the fennel. Drizzle on any remaining oil and bake in a preheated oven at 200°C/400°F/Gas 6, for 20-30 minutes.

The fennel is cooked when the heart is soft and the outside a light golden brown. Remove the vegetables to a serving dish and lay the pepper strips across them. Drizzle on any pan juices and oil, sprinkle over the thyme and serve at room temperature.

Broccoli salad with sesame seeds and balsamic vinegar

SERVES 4

6 sun-dried tomato halves
450 g (1 lb) fresh broccoli (trimmed weight)
2 tablespoons olive oil
2 tablespoons sesame seeds
1 clove garlic, crushed and chopped
1 teaspoon balsamic vinegar
sea salt and black pepper

If the sun-dried tomatoes are not packed in oil, soak for a few minutes in warm water. Slice into strips.

Cut the broccoli into smallish pieces and cook in rapidly boiling water for 2-3 minutes. Drain and plunge into a bowl of iced water. Leave to cool. Remove from the water and drain on kitchen towels.

Heat the oil and fry the sesame seeds for 60 seconds, then add the garlic and cook for a further minute.

Place the broccoli in a serving dish and pour over the hot oil, scraping all the seeds and garlic out of the pan. Scatter on the tomatoes, then drizzle over the balsamic vinegar. Toss gently. Taste and correct the seasoning, then serve at room temperature.

Marinated Shallots

Serve this dish with a selection of other salads, or as an accompaniment to grilled meat or fish. It can be made a day in advance.

SERVES 4-6

450 g (1 lb) shallots or pickling onoins
200 g (7 oz) tin chopped tomatoes
60 g (2 oz) raisins
1 tablespoon olive oil
2-3 tablespoons wine vinegar
140 ml (¼ pint) water
1 teaspoon chopped herbs
1 clove garlic, crushed
1 bay leaf
sea salt and black pepper

Peel the shallots and place in a pan of cold water. Bring to the boil and simmer for 2 minutes, then drain and return to the pan. Add the remaining ingredients and add a little extra water if needed to cover the onions.

Bring to the boil and simmer over a low heat for about 30 minutes, or until the onions are tender. Allow to cool, then serve at room temperature.

CARROT AND NUT SALAD IN A POPPYSEED DRESSING

Poppyseeds look good in salad dressings and give a wonderful texture and taste to the salad. Use only firm young carrots that are full of flavour.

SERVES 4

60 g (2 oz) sultanas
450 g (1 lb) carrots
4 tablespoons chopped mixed nuts

FOR THE DRESSING
1 tablespoon olive oil
2 tablespoons groundnut or light vegetable oil
1 tablespoon clear honey
1 tablespoon wine vinegar
sea salt and black pepper
1 tablespoon poppyseeds
1 tablespoon chopped chives

Cover the sultanas with a little warm water and leave for 5-10 minutes to plump up. Meanwhile, coarsely grate the carrots. Drain the sultanas and mix with the carrots and nuts.

Mix the dressing ingredients by shaking them together in a screw-topped jar, and pour over the salad. Toss everything together to coat well with the dressing.

GREEK SALAD

Traditional Greek salad can be served on its own with bread, or as a side dish to accompany grilled meat.

SERVES 4

170 g (6 oz) feta cheese, cubed
½ cucumber, sliced
340 g (12 oz) firm ripe tomatoes, sliced
1 medium onion, sliced
115 g (4 oz) pitted black olives
1 teaspoon fresh marjoram leaves
2-3 tablespoons Greek Olive oil
black pepper

Mix the cheese, cucumber, tomatoes, onion and olives in a bowl. Add the marjoram, then drizzle over the oil and season with pepper. Feta cheese can be very salty, so salt may not be necessary.

ADUKI BEAN, RED AND YELLOW PEPPER SALAD

Soak the aduki beans overnight and then simmer in plenty of fresh water until soft.
Alternatively, place the beans in a deep pan, cover well with water and bring to the
boil. Boil rapidly for 2 minutes, then cover the pan and leave to sit for 1 hour. Bring
the beans back to the boil and simmer until tender.

SERVES 6

225 g (8 oz) cooked aduki beans (see above)
1 red and 1 yellow pepper, diced
4 ribs celery, diced
4 spring onions, sliced
3 tablespoons each chopped fresh dill and parsley

FOR THE DRESSING
4 tablespoons olive oil
1 tablespoon red wine vinegar
1 teaspoon Dijon mustard
sea salt and black pepper

Mix the dressing ingredients together by shaking them in a screw-topped
jar. Drain the cooked beans well and toss with 3-4 tablespoons of dressing.
Allow to cool.

Add the vegetables and herbs, toss well with the remaining dressing,
then taste and correct the seasoning.

TROPICAL FRUIT AND COTTAGE CHEESE SALAD WITH POPPYSEED DRESSING

This is a recipe full of contrasting tastes and textures. It makes a delicious light lunch or supper and is delightfully low in calories. Use peaches, ripe pears and nectarines if available, and substitute flat-leaf parsley for the chives in the poppyseed dressing on page 119.

SERVES 4

1 small ripe pineapple
1 ripe mango
1 ripe papaya
2 red skinned apples
1 tablespoon lemon juice
crisp lettuce leaves
450 g (1 lb) natural cottage cheese
poppyseed dressing (page 119)

Peel and core the pineapple and mango. Cut the flesh into 2.5 cm (1 inch) dice and place in a bowl. Peel the papaya and remove the seeds, dice the flesh and add to the other fruit. Core, but don't peel the apples, dice and toss in a little lemon juice, then add to the bowl. Toss the fruit to mix.

Arrange a bed of lettuce leaves on a shallow serving dish and heap the fruit on top. Spoon on the cottage cheese.

Mix the dressing ingredients together and taste. Correct the seasoning, then drizzle over the salad.

CAESAR SALAD

Caesar salad is said to have been the invention of necessity. When the Caesar's Palace restaurant in Los Angeles had a sudden and unforeseen arrival of dinner guests, Caesar Cardini gathered together the ingredients he had in the kitchen and, in the spirit of all great chefs, created a dish to fit the occasion.

I use a hardboiled egg yolk rather than a raw egg in the dressing, and rustic or French bread rather than sliced white.

SERVES 2 OR 4

6 slices day-old white bread
olive oil for frying
1 head Cos lettuce
1 small head soft lettuce
4-6 anchovy fillets, chopped
60 g (2 oz) fresh parmesan, flaked

FOR THE DRESSING
1 clove garlic, crushed
½ teaspoon Dijon mustard
yolk of 1 hardboiled egg
1 tablespoon lemon juice
sea salt and black pepper
2 tablespoons white wine vinegar
140 ml (¼ pint) olive oil
2 tablespoons freshly grated parmesan

Cut the bread into cubes and fry in olive oil until golden. Place the dressing ingredients in a blender and process until smooth and creamy.

Arrange the torn salad leaves in a large bowl and scatter on the anchovies, the croûtons and the parmesan flakes. Just before serving pour on the dressing and toss well.

SALAD NIÇOISE

This salad always reminds me of the time I shared a flat with friends while we were working as nurses in London. Shash, who couldn't even follow the instructions on a packet of instant whip, often made the most wonderful salade niçoise.

SERVES 4

1 medium head soft lettuce
4 hardboiled eggs, quartered
1 tin tuna in oil, drained and flaked
4-6 firm, ripe tomatoes, quartered
4-6 anchovy fillets
115 g (4 oz) green beans, sliced, cooked and cooled
1 red onion, finely sliced
60 g (2 oz) pitted black olives

FOR THE DRESSING
6 tablespoons olive oil
2 tablespoons red wine vinegar
sea salt and black pepper
½ teaspoon Dijon mustard
1 clove garlic, crushed and finely chopped

Place the lettuce in the base of a large bowl and arrange the other ingredients on top. Mix the dressing ingredients together by shaking in a screw-topped jar, and drizzle over the salad.

AMERICAN POTATO SALAD

The climate in America encourages picnics, barbecues and cook-outs and there is always a bowl of rich, creamy potato salad served alongside the grilled meat. The secret of this salad lies in making the dressing in two stages.

SERVES 6

900 g (2 lb) waxy old potatoes
2 tablespoons olive oil
1 tablespoon wine vinegar
sea salt and black pepper
225 g (8 oz) streaky bacon, derinded and chopped
1 green pepper, diced
1 bunch salad onions, sliced
2 ribs celery, chopped
2 hardboiled eggs, chopped
2 tablespoons chopped parsley

FOR THE DRESSING
140 ml (¼ pint) soured cream
140 ml (¼ pint) mayonnaise
2 tablespoons wholegrain mustard
2 tablespoons chopped dill

Peel the potatoes and cook in plenty of salted water until tender, but still firm. Drain and place in a bowl. Cut into cubes while they are still hot. Mix the oil with the vinegar, and gently toss the potatoes in this dressing. Season and leave to cool. Fry the bacon in its own fat until crisp. Drain on kitchen paper.

Mix together the soured cream dressing ingredients. When the potatoes are cool, stir in the pepper, onions, celery, eggs and bacon, then gently mix in the soured cream dressing. Spoon into a serving bowl and garnish with the parsley.

Spinach salad

The tiniest brilliant green leaves of spinach and sweet cherry tomatoes are the chief ingredients of this salad. Spinach keeps its crunch and colour better than lettuce, so this makes a good salad for a buffet.

SERVES 4

**450 g (1 lb) young spinach leaves
225 g (8 oz) cherry tomatoes**

FOR THE DRESSING
**1 tablespoon red wine vinegar
2 tablespoons olive oil
1 tablespoon tomato ketchup
1 teaspoon clear honey
good dash of Tabasco
lemon juice to taste
sea salt and black pepper**

Carefully wash the spinach leaves in several changes of cold water. Always lift the leaves from the water to allow any sand to sink to the bottom of the bowl. Spin the clean leaves dry and tear away any coarse stems.

Cut the tomatoes into quarters. Arrange the spinach and tomatoes in a large bowl. Mix the dressing ingredients together and pour over the salad. Toss well just before serving.

Bulgur salad

Bulgur is a delicious vegetarian dish with enough taste to satisfy meat-eaters too. This salad improves if made a couple of hours in advance. It travels well and can be eaten with crisp lettuce leaf scoops. Leftover roast chicken, chunks of ham or cheese can also be added.

Serves 6

340 g (12 oz) bulgur
1 litre (1½ pints) water
5 tablespoons olive oil
juice and grated zest of 1 large lemon
sea salt and black pepper
1 large red pepper, diced
2 onions, finely chopped
½ cucumber, peeled and diced
1-2 plump cloves garlic, crushed and finely chopped
400 g (14 oz) tin chickpeas, drained
60 g (2 oz) walnut kernels, finely chopped
3-4 firm ripe tomatoes, plum tomatoes for preference
wine vinegar to taste
1 bunch parsley, chopped
1 bunch coriander, chopped

Put the bulgur into a large bowl and pour on the water. Stir to mix, then leave to soak for about 45 minutes. Drain, then press out as much excess water as possible with your hands.

Add the oil, lemon juice and zest, salt and pepper and toss well. Add the red pepper, onions, cucumber, garlic, chickpeas, walnuts and tomatoes, and toss everything together well. Taste the salad; at this stage you may need to add more oil, some vinegar and extra salt or pepper. Allow to rest for a couple of hours, then finally, sprinkle on the herbs.

WILD RICE SALAD WITH PINE NUTS AND BLACK OLIVES

The wild rice and olives look exotic against the white rice and pine nuts. Long-grain rice and wild rice can be bought mixed in a packet, or weigh out separate quantities as below. Hazelnuts can be substituted for pine nuts. I like to serve this salad with beef, as the flavour and texture marry well with red meat.

Sometimes I add a finely chopped red chilli and a spoonful of chilli oil to this recipe.

SERVES 6

225 g (8 oz) long-grain rice
60 g (2 oz) wild rice
4 tablespoons extra virgin olive oil
1 tablespoon red wine vinegar
sea salt and black pepper
60 g (2 oz) pine nuts
1 large clove garlic, crushed and finely chopped
85 g (3 oz) pitted black olives, roughly chopped
2 tablespoons chopped chives
juice and zest of ½ lemon

Cook the rice in plenty of boiling water. Wild rice takes about 40 minutes, long-grain rice 15-20 minutes, or follow the instructions on the packet.

Drain the rice and, while it is still hot, add 1 tablespoon each of oil and the wine vinegar, and season with salt and pepper.

Heat the remaining oil in a frying pan and cook the pine nuts until they begin to colour. Add the garlic and cook for a further minute. Pour this over the rice.

Add the olives, chives and lemon zest. Taste and correct the seasoning with lemon juice.

Best bean salad

This is a salad that can take on a dozen or more different flavours. Add tuna chunks, avocado, mozzarella, chopped chicken, ham or garlic sausage and it makes a good main-course dish. Chopped walnuts, peanuts and raisins suit vegetarians. Chopped fresh coriander and chilli give it a Mexican flavour. Served plain, it makes an excellent accompaniment to grilled sausages.

Cook the beans separately to keep the colours true and make sure each variety is done to perfection.

Serves 4-6

85 g (3 oz) each red, black and white beans
4 spring onions, finely chopped
2 tablespoons chopped parsley

For the dressing
4-6 tablespoons oil
1 tablespoon wine vinegar
pinch sugar
sea salt and black pepper

Keeping the varieties separate, wash the beans and bring them to the boil in plenty of water. Simmer for 2 minutes then take the pans from the heat and leave for 1 hour. Return the beans to the boil and cook until tender. Drain and allow to cool.

Mix the onions and parsley with the beans. Combine the oil, vinegar and seasoning, and pour over the dressing. Add extra ingredients as suggested above if you like, tasting the salad and adding more dressing if needed.

DICED AUBERGINE SALAD

This is a lovely salad to serve with barbecued lamb or chicken kebabs, or as a first course with hot Arab bread.

SERVES 4-6

2 medium aubergines
sea salt and black pepper
olive oil for frying
1 teaspoon marjoram leaves
1 clove garlic, crushed and finely chopped
½ teaspoon honey
2 tablespoons wine vinegar
2 tablespoons chopped flat-leaf parsley

Cut off the top and a small slice from the bottom of each aubergine and discard. Dice the aubergine, place in a colander and sprinkle liberally with salt. Leave for 1 hour to sweat. Rinse the cubes well under running cold water, then pat dry with kitchen paper.

Heat about 5 mm (¼ inch) olive oil in a frying pan and when hot, fry the aubergines in single-layer batches, adding a little marjoram with each batch. Turn often until soft and lightly coloured, then remove to a dish. Fry the garlic with the last batch of aubergine for 1-2 minutes. Spoon away and discard excess oil that drains from the aubergines.

Mix the honey into the vinegar and sprinkle this over the aubergines. Season with pepper, and salt if needed. Scatter on the parsley and serve at room temperature.

WARM CHICKEN AND HERB SALAD

This is a wonderful summer dish. I saw it prepared at the Cordon Bleu Cooking School in Paris where the chef used rabbit in place of chicken. Bone the chicken breasts yourself, and use the bones in the stock. If you wish to use rabbit, ask the butcher to bone the loin and the legs, then use the trimming plus the shoulders to make the stock.

SERVES 6

6 chicken breasts, boned, skin on
good bunch each fresh tarragon, chives, parsley and dill
olive oil

FOR THE STOCK
2 tablespoons olive oil
1 onion, finely chopped
1 carrot, finely chopped
bones from the chicken breasts
1 clove garlic, finely chopped
stems from herbs
salt and pepper

FOR THE DRESSING
2 tablespoons sherry vinegar
4 tablespoons olive oil

TO FINISH
a selection of baby salad and herb leaves
1 Cos lettuce, finely sliced
6 ripe plum tomatoes, peeled and sliced

Heat the oil for the stock in a saucepan and fry the onion and carrot until coloured. Add the chicken bones and fry until lightly browned. Add the garlic and herb stems and cover with about 275 ml (½ pint) water. Season lightly and simmer, adding more water if necessary. Cook the stock for 30 minutes, then strain and reserve. You should have about 140 ml (¼ pint) stock.

Lay the chicken breasts skin side down on a board and cover with a piece of cling film, then beat them lightly with a mallet or heavy saucepan to flatten slightly. Divide the herb leaves between them and season with salt and pepper.

Roll up the breasts to form sausage shapes and tie with string or secure with cocktail sticks. Put the breasts in a roasting dish and drizzle with a little oil. Cook in a preheated oven at 190°C/375°F/Gas 5 for 20-25 minutes, or until golden brown. Remove from the pan and reserve.

Place the roasting dish on the hob over a moderate heat and add the sherry vinegar. Stir well to deglaze, then pour the contents of the dish into a saucepan. Add the stock and the oil. Boil rapidly for 3-4 minutes to reduce and amalgamate the dressing.

Meanwhile, divide the salad between 6 plates. Place a ring of tomato slices around the edge. Remove the string or cocktail sticks, and carve the chicken breasts into medallions. Arrange these in the centre of the salad, then spoon over the boiling dressing and serve at once.

SMOKED CHICKEN SALAD WITH HONEY YOGHURT DRESSING

This main course salad makes a delicious change from Coronation chicken. Here smoked chicken is served dressed with a sharp and sweet yoghurt-based sauce. Green grapes or fresh peaches can be used instead of apples.

SERVES 4-5

1 smoked chicken
2 crisp eating apples
lemon juice
1 iceberg or other crisp lettuce
3 ribs celery, chopped
3 tablespoons roasted peanuts
chopped chives and chervil

FOR THE DRESSING
140 ml (¼ pint) thick set natural yoghurt
1 tablespoon clear honey
sea salt and black pepper
lemon juice to taste
½ teaspoon sweet paprika

Take all the chicken from the carcass and discard the bones. Cut the meat into large chunks. Core and dice the apples, and brush with lemon juice. Shred the lettuce and arrange on a serving platter. Mix the dressing ingredients together by shaking in a screw-topped jar.

Pile the chicken, celery, apples and nuts on to the lettuce and drizzle over the dressing. Scatter on the chopped herbs and serve with tiny new potatoes or fresh bread.

CRUDITÉS

Crisp young vegetables are served raw – either whole or cut into batons with a pot of homemade mayonnaise, or grated and individually dressed. Choose vegetables with good bite and colour and arrange them attractively on a large platter, with the dressed grated vegetables in lines. The range of vegetables suitable for crudités is almost endless, and includes carrots, green beans, red peppers, baby corns, celery, broccoli, radishes with their leaves, and courgettes. For mayonnaise, see below, or choose one of the other dressings in this chapter.

Always serve good bread with crudités.

MAYONNAISE

I love the classic raw-egg mayonnaise, though after the scares of recent years you may prefer not to give it to anyone with a delicate constitution.

140 ml (¼ pint) light olive oil
2-3 tablespoons extra virgin oil
2 egg yolks
1 scant tablespoon wine vinegar
½ teaspoon mustard powder
fine table salt and white pepper

Combine the oils in a jug, and mix the yolks, vinegar and mustard in a food processor. With the motor running slowly, pour the oil into the egg mixture, almost drop by drop. As the sauce begins to thicken, pour the oil more rapidly, increasing to a thin stream. Once all the oil is incorporated, taste and check the seasoning.

Very thick mayonnaise can be thinned by adding a little single cream, again with the motor running.

GARLIC MAYONNAISE OR AÏOLI

A thick pungent sauce traditionally eaten in the south of France and Spain, aïoli can be used as a salad dressing or a dip for crudités, or be spooned into chilled soups. It can be made in a food processor or in the more traditional way with a pestle and mortar.

4 plump cloves fresh garlic
sea salt and white pepper
2 teaspoons wine vinegar
1 teaspoon Dijon mustard
2 size 2 egg yolks
140 ml (¼ pint) olive oil

Crush the garlic and salt to a paste or process until well chopped. Add the vinegar, mustard and egg yolks and then, processing slowly all the while, start adding the oil drop by drop until the emulsion 'takes'. Pour in the oil a little faster, but still only in the thinnest stream. When all the oil has been incorporated, taste the mayonnaise and correct the seasoning.

Allow to rest for several hours before serving, to let the flavours develop fully.

Smoked garlic, available from specialist food stores, can be used instead of fresh garlic in this recipe.

THOUSAND ISLAND DRESSING

This American classic gets its name from the coloured bits that float like islands in the sauce. It keeps for at least a week stored in a covered jar in the fridge.

2 tablespoons tomato purée
2 tablespoons tomato ketchup
140 ml (¼ pint) mayonnaise
140 ml (¼ pint) buttermilk or single cream
2 tablespoons wine vinegar
1 hardboiled egg, chopped
2 tablespoons chopped gherkins
2 tablespoons chopped red pepper
1 tablespoon chopped chives
sea salt and black pepper

Beat together the tomato purée, ketchup, mayonnaise, buttermilk or cream and vinegar. Fold in the remaining ingredients, and season to taste.

BLUE CHEESE DRESSING

275 ml (½ pint) mayonnaise
140 ml (¼ pint) soured cream
1 clove garlic, crushed
1 tablespoon Dijon mustard
2 tablespoons vegetable oil
1 tablespoon wine vinegar
115 g (4 oz) blue cheese, crumbled

Beat together all the ingredients except the cheese, then stir this in. Allow the dressing to stand for an hour before serving.

SAUCE MARIE ROSE

This is a delicious pretty pink dressing and much maligned in my experience.

4 tablespoons double cream
6 tablespoons mayonnaise, homemade for preference
3 tablespoons tomato ketchup
1 clove garlic, crushed and finely chopped
fine table salt and white pepper
lemon juice to taste

Whip the cream until it just holds its shape, then fold in the remaining ingredients, adding lemon juice to taste.

SOURED CREAM AND MUSTARD DRESSING

This is a good sauce for potato salad and can also be spooned over boiled new potatoes.

140 ml (¼ pint) soured cream
2 tablespoons wholegrain mustard
fine table salt and black pepper

Beat the cream with the mustard and season to taste. Allow to rest for 1 hour for the flavour to develop before serving.

CREAMY AVOCADO DRESSING

Like all avocado dishes, this lovely light green dressing should be used as soon as possible after it has been made to avoid discoloration.

1 ripe avocado
140 ml (¼ pint) soured cream
1 tablespoon finely chopped onion
2 tablespoons lemon juice
1 clove garlic, crushed and finely chopped
1 tablespoon chopped parsley
fine table salt and white pepper

Peel the avocado and remove the stone. Place all the ingredients in a blender and process until smooth. Season to taste.

FROMAGE FRAIS DRESSING

Use a full flavoured olive oil in this dressing for maximum flavour and minimum calories. It is delicious spooned on to finely sliced bulb fennel and ripe tomatoes.

2 tablespoons lemon juice
1 tablespoon extra virgin olive oil
1 tablespoon cold water
140 ml (¼ pint) very low fat fromage frais
2 tablespoons each chopped mint and chives
fine table salt and white pepper

Beat the lemon juice, oil and water into the fromage frais, then fold in the herbs and season to taste.

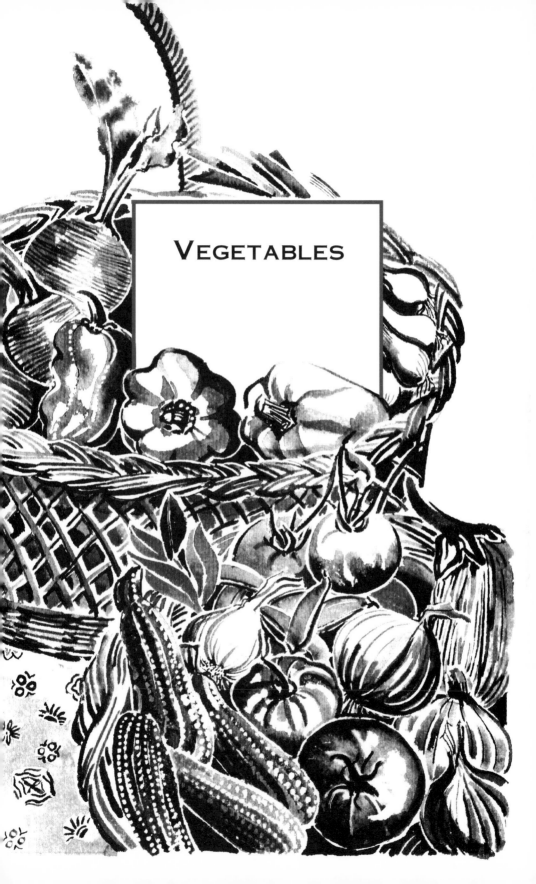

VEGETABLES

For me, the best part of summer is the fresh taste of garden vegetables. And even though I am a city dweller, the produce available from my local market tastes all the better from having been picked in nearby Kent or Sussex and not transported half way across Europe in a refrigerated van.

While my garden is limited to the growing of fresh herbs, rocket for salads and a couple of apple trees, I know from frequent trips to pick-your-own farms and friends' more prolific gardens that there are two sides to nature's bountiful harvest. It is a sorry truth that just when your own courgettes are at their most productive you will never pass a friend's house without being offered more of the same. The same is true for apples, vegetable marrows, runner beans… Why is it that every time I walk out into a field of peas, beans, strawberries, rhubarb, asparagus etc., I suffer from the most overpowering and crippling amnesia? As my eyes glimpse the treasure trove I immediately forget the size not only of my family but also the freezer and in extreme cases the carrying capacity of my car! How many times have I staggered home with a boot full of vegetables and fruit, exhausted from the unaccustomed work of the harvest and had to spend most of the night preparing my bounty for freezing and pickling only to find when I reach the freezer that last year's crop is still there sitting untouched in its clearly-labelled polythene bags?

The moral to this tale is that food tastes best when fresh and while you want to store excess beware of always eating last year's frozen vegetables in order to make room for this year's!

Most summer vegetables need little preparation and only the lightest cooking to bring out their delicate flavours. To enjoy them at their best, eat them as soon as possible after picking or buying. Always put green vegetables into boiling water and cook only until they begin to become tender.

• **Garden peas.** Who doesn't love peas straight from the pod? I have wonderful memories of standing in my father's vegetable garden picking pods of tiny peas and hiding the evidence in the compost heap. Always shell the peas just before you need them and cook in plenty of very lightly salted water. (I prefer not to add sugar or mint to the water but many do.) Boil over a high heat for 3-4 minutes then drain and toss with butter. Serve at once.

• **Courgettes** have too delicate a taste to be boiled, so steam them over a pan of simmering water for about 5 minutes. To serve, toss in butter and sprinkle on a little chopped parsley. Try to pick them very small and eat them fresh from the plant.

• **Spinach** is another vegetable that I feel should never be cooked in water. I've given my favourite recipes in this chapter.

• **Broad beans.** These must be among my very favourite vegetables. I love to eat them when they are tiny, often adding them to a simple parmesan-flavoured risotto. Shell and cook as for peas, tossing in melted butter or extra virgin olive oil.

• **Runner beans.** The British, it is said, are hopelessly devoted to runner beans. I have seldom seen this variety of bean outside the United Kingdom and so perhaps there is some truth in this. They must be eaten before they develop their thick inner skin and stringy sides. Pick them young about 15-20 cm (6-8 inches) in length and, having topped and tailed them, slice by hand into thin pieces. Boil in lightly salted water for 2-3 minutes and toss with butter.

• **French beans** are delicious cooked in a little olive oil with some garlic until tender-crisp. They are also good lightly boiled, then cooled and added to salads.

• **Samphire.** One of my earliest memories is of collecting samphire from the salt marshes along the north Norfolk coast. We would trudge home along the beach carring our harvest, and then spend hours washing it under running water to remove the mountains of sand and mud that clung to each stem. We ate it boiled for about 5 minutes in unsalted water and served with melted butter, like asparagus. Steamed samphire is delicious with light fish such as plaice, especially when served with beurre blanc. Preserve any surplus samphire by covering with boiling wine vinegar spiced with a few peppercorns and a dried chilli.

• **Sweetcorn.** Small-kernelled and sweet, pale white cobs of corn are a lasting memory of the years lived in North America. It was there I learned to cook this delicious vegetable.

Cook sweetcorn, peeled of all its leaves, in a pan of fast-boiling unsalted water until it smells ready - which should be in 7-10 minutes. Drain and serve with melted butter and plenty of salt and pepper. If there are only a few people eating, corncobs cook very well in the microwave. Leave on all the leaves and silk, cook on full power for 8 minutes for one or 12 minutes for two, then allow to cool for 60 seconds before stripping off the leaves.

• **Beetroot.** The delicate flavour of beetroot is often murdered by the awful habit of drenching it in malt vinegar. Though it's usually eaten only as a garnish, properly treated, it is a lovely vegetable in its own right and delicious served hot. I have included two recipes for this undeservedly neglected vegetable (see pages 144 and 145).

• **Aubergine.** The aubergine is a vegetable that is associated with much superstition and folk lore. Thought at one time to bring ill luck, it was banned from tables in France and Italy. These days we love the rather elusive flavour and silky texture of aubergines and eat them in a variety of ways. Many recipes will tell you to sweat the sliced vegetable, sprinkling the cut surfaces with salt and leaving them to sit until the bitter brown juices run. This is not strictly necessary if time is short, especially when the aubergine is fresh and of a small to medium size.

• **Potatoes.** New potatoes are quite wonderful. Small and waxy, the taste is quite sublime and when cooking the first potatoes I would only ever consider boiling in salted water and serving with butter. Once the season is well established I roast new potatoes in their skins, cooking them in a mixture of olive oil, herbs and coarse salt.

BRAISED PEAS WITH LETTUCE

This is a good recipe for those slightly bigger garden peas.

SERVES 6

30 g (1 oz) butter
1 shallot, finely chopped
450 g (1 lb) peas (shelled weight)
4-5 large lettuce leaves, roughly torn
140 ml (¼ pint) chicken stock
sea salt and black pepper

Melt the butter in a saucepan and fry the shallot until soft but not coloured. Add the peas and lettuce leaves and cook for 2-3 minutes, turning everything in the butter.

Add the stock and simmer for 7-10 minutes until the peas are very tender and most of the liquid has evaporated. Check the seasoning and serve.

SAUTÉED COURGETTES

SERVES 6

450 g (1 lb) small firm courgettes
1 tablespoon olive oil
30 g (1 oz) butter
1-2 plump cloves garlic, crushed
sea salt and black pepper
lemon juice

Trim the ends from the courgettes and cut into batons.

Heat the oil and butter in a large frying pan and stir-fry the courgettes. When they begin to wilt, add the garlic, and cook over a high heat until the courgettes are golden. Serve at once, seasoned with salt, pepper and a squeeze of lemon juice.

COURGETTE FRITTERS

These are not tiny individual fritters, but more of a nest of golden crisp courgette sticks to pull apart at the table.

SERVES 4

340 g (12 oz) firm courgettes
sea salt, black pepper and nutmeg
85 g (3 oz) plain flour
2 egg whites
oil for frying
2-3 large basil leaves, torn into pieces

Cut the courgettes into batons. Season the flour very well and tip into a plastic bag. In a large bowl, whisk the egg whites until stiff. Heat the oil.

Dampen the courgettes with a little water, then toss in the flour. Empty the contents of the bag into the egg whites and fold together. Lifting the courgettes out with two forks, fry in batches in a single layer, turning as necessary, until golden brown. Keep warm until you have fried the rest and serve at once sprinkled with basil.

KOHLRABI WITH RED PEPPERS

This underrated relative of the cabbage comes in red, green and purple. The tuberous stem is the part you eat. I like to stir-fry fine sticks of kohlrabi and serve them with grilled meat or fish.

SERVES 4

2 medium kohlrabi
2 tablespoons olive oil
1 red pepper, cut into batons
sea salt and black pepper

Peel the kohlrabi stems and cut into sticks. Heat the oil in a wok and stir-fry the vegetables for 4-5 minutes or until they are cooked but still crisp. Season with salt and pepper and serve at once.

WILTED SPINACH

SERVES 4

**450 g (1 lb) young spinach leaves
2-3 tablespoons butter
salt, pepper and nutmeg**

Wash the spinach well, shaking off most but not all of the water. Place the clean leaves in a large pan over a moderate heat. Press the leaves down as they wilt, turning from time to time.

After 2-3 minutes, when they are very soft, turn the leaves into a colander and press with a spoon to squeeze out as much liquid as possible.

Melt the butter in the saucepan, return the spinach and toss over a high heat. Season to taste with salt, pepper and a little grated nutmeg and serve at once.

STIR-FRIED SPINACH WITH SPRING ONIONS

SERVES 4

**450 g (1 lb) baby spinach leaves
1 tablespoon olive oil
1 tablespoon sesame seeds
1 bunch spring onions, cut into batons
sea salt and black pepper**

Wash and dry the spinach.

Heat the oil in a large frying pan and cook the sesame seeds until they start to pop. Now add the onions and cook until they wilt. Add the spinach and stir-fry over a high heat until it wilts and all the water is driven off.

Season to taste with salt and pepper and serve at once.

FRENCH BEAN AND EGG SALAD

SERVES 4

450 g (1 lb) young french beans
2 hardboiled eggs

FOR THE DRESSING
3 tablespoons light olive oil
1 tablespoon white wine vinegar
pinch each mustard and sugar
salt and pepper

Top and tail the beans and cook in plenty of boiling salted water for
3 minutes. Drain and plunge into iced water to cool. Remove from the
water and pat dry with kitchen paper. Arrange on a serving dish.

Cut the eggs in half and remove and reserve the yolks. Chop the egg
whites and scatter over the beans.

Mix the dressing ingredients together and season to taste. Pour over
the beans.

Put the egg yolks in a sieve and press down with a wooden spoon to
sieve them over the beans. Serve chilled.

BEETROOT WITH SOURED CREAM AND DILL

SERVES 4-6

6 medium beetroot
140 ml (¼ pint) soured cream
a little milk
2 tablespoons chopped dill
salt and pepper

Boil the beetroot in plenty of lightly salted water for 30-40 minutes until
tender. Allow to cool, then slip off the skins and slice the beets into rounds.
Put them in a greased ovenproof dish.

Beat the cream with about 2 tablespoons milk and add the dill and
seasoning.

Pour over the beetroot and cook in a preheated oven at 180°C/360°F/
Gas 4 for 20-25 minutes.

Serve hot with chicken, pork or fish.

ROAST BEETROOT WITH ORANGE AND GARLIC

SERVES 6

**6-8 medium beetroot
2 tablespoons olive oil
1-2 plump cloves of garlic
grated zest and juice of 1 large orange
salt and black pepper**

Boil the beets for 30-40 minutes in plenty of lightly salted water until tender, then allow to cool and slip off the skins. Cut each beet into quarters.

Mix the remaining ingredients in an ovenproof dish and toss in the beetroot. Roast in a preheated oven at 180°C/360°F/Gas 4 for 25-30 minutes.

Serve with chicken, pork or game.

AUBERGINE SALAD

SERVES 4-6

**2 medium aubergines or 6-8 baby aubergines
salt and black pepper
olive oil for frying
1 shallot, finely chopped
2-3 sprigs fresh thyme
2 cloves garlic
2 tablespoons balsamic vinegar
140 ml (¼ pint) natural yoghurt (optional)**

Cut the aubergine into 2 cm (¾ inch) dice and sprinkle with salt. Leave for 30 minutes then rinse well under running water to remove as much salt as possible. Pat dry on kitchen paper.

Heat about 6 tablespoons of oil in a frying pan and cook the aubergines, turning often until they start to soften. Add the shallot, thyme and garlic and continue cooking until everything is a light golden brown. Turn off the heat. Season with black pepper and add the balsamic vinegar to the hot contents of the pan.

Allow the mixture to cool, then spoon into a serving dish, scraping in any pan juices. Top the salad with natural yoghurt if desired.

This salad is good served with hot pitta bread.

LAYERED MEDITERRANEAN VEGETABLES

Much as I like traditional ratatouille (see page 149), I sometimes think the flavour is a little muddled. So I make this ratatouille-inspired dish, frying each component individually and then layering them, before finally baking gently in the oven to allow the flavours to melt into each other.

SERVES 4

1 medium aubergine
sea salt and black pepper
2 large ripe tomatoes
1 red pepper
olive oil for frying
1 red onion, sliced
2-3 medium courgettes, cut into batons
1 clove garlic, crushed
1-2 tablespoons balsamic vinegar
fresh basil leaves

Slice the aubergine into thin rounds and sprinkle with salt. Leave to drain for 30 minutes, rinse well and pat dry.

Skin the tomatoes by dipping in boiling water and peel the red pepper with a sharp knife or a potato peeler.

Starting with the aubergines and omitting the tomatoes, fry the vegetables individually, cooking only as many as the pan can hold in a single layer. As they are cooked, layer them in a smallish ovenproof dish. Lay the raw tomato slices on top.

Check you have about 2 tablespoons oil in the pan and fry the garlic until pale gold. Add the balsamic vinegar, stir well, then spoon the juices over the vegetables. Cook in a moderate oven at 180°C/360°F/Gas 4 for about 20 minutes.

Serve warm or cold, garnished with basil.

Ragoût of new vegetables

*This wonderfully fresh tasting ragoût is based on a dish made at Gidleigh Park,
Chagford, Devon by the talented chef Shaun Hill. It is perfect as a light lunch or
starter, and the quantities given are a guide only. The sauce serves 6. It is better to
use a liquidizer than a food processor for making the sauce.*

SERVES 4

8 small carrots
8 spring onions or baby leeks
4 runner beans
8 asparagus spears
8 small courgettes
115 g (4 oz) shelled peas
1 clove garlic
salt
225 g (8 oz) oyster or button mushrooms
1 tablespoon oil for frying

FOR THE SAUCE
200 ml (⅓ pint) vegetable cooking water
1 tablespoon crème fraîche (optional)
60 g (2 oz) peccorino or parmesan cheese
handful fresh basil leaves
black pepper
squeeze of lemon juice
140 ml (¼ pint) good olive oil

Prepare the vegetables. Bring a scant 600 ml (1 pint) water to the boil, add
the garlic clove and salt lightly. Start cooking the vegetables, adding them
to the pot so they will all be cooked at the same time: first the carrots, then
the onions etc. The total cooking time should be about 8 minutes.

Remove the vegetables from the water with a slotted spoon and keep
warm. Meanwhile, fry the mushrooms in the oil until golden and keep
warm.

To make the sauce, put the vegetable cooking water plus the garlic
clove in a liquidizer and add the crème fraîche, cheese, basil, pepper and
lemon juice. Whizz until combined.

With the motor still running, add the olive oil in a thin stream.
Continue to whizz until the mixture is well amalgamated.

Divide the vegetables between warmed serving bowls and spoon over
the sauce. Serve at once.

HERB-ROAST NEW POTATOES WITH ROASTED GARLIC

SERVES 6

675 g (1½ lb) new potatoes
4-6 tablespoons olive oil
1 tablespoon chopped mixed herbs
sea salt and black pepper
1 head or 10-15 cloves fresh pink skinned garlic (optional)

Wash and dry the potatoes. Put the oil, herbs, salt and pepper in a roasting dish and add the potatoes. Separate the garlic cloves but do not remove the skins.

Toss the potatoes and garlic in the oil mixture and roast in a hot oven at 200°C/400°F/Gas 6 for 30-40 minutes, depending on size. The potatoes are ready when crisp on the outside and soft all through.

DÉLICE PARMENTIER

New crop King Edwards are good in this lovely soothing spring dish that I first ate in Paris.

SERVES 4-6

450 g (1 lb) new potatoes
140 ml (¼ pint) double cream
sea salt and black pepper
salmon roe or caviar

Wash and dry the potatoes and bake in a preheated oven at 200°C/400°F/ Gas 6 for about 20 minutes or until soft. Remove from the oven and allow to cool slightly. Slice each potato in half lengthways and carefully scrape out the contents with a small spoon, leaving potato 'boats'.

Mash the removed potato with just enough cream to give a smooth texture and a rich taste. Season with salt and pepper. Pile the potato back into the 'boats' on individual plates. Reheat just before serving, then top each hot potato with a dash of cream and some caviar or salmon roe. Serve at once.

PROVENÇALE TOMATO TART

A lovely way to serve those ripest, flavour-packed summer tomatoes, this tart is best eaten the day it is made.

SERVES 6

225 g (8 oz) ready-made puff pastry
4 tablespoons olive oil
85 g (3 oz) day-old white breadcrumbs
1 plump clove garlic, crushed
2 tablespoons finely chopped parsley
1 kg (2¼ lb) ripe tomatoes
2 tablespoons herb-flavoured French mustard
sea salt and black pepper

Roll out the pastry to fit a swiss roll tin and chill. Heat half the oil in a frying pan and fry the breadcrumbs until golden, adding the garlic just before they are ready. Mix in the parsley.

Slice the tomatoes thinly, discarding any excess juice. Spread the mustard on the pastry, then arrange the tomato slices on top. Sprinkle over the crumbs and season. Drizzle on the remaining oil.

Bake the tart in a hot oven at 200°C/400°F/Gas 6 for 20-30 minutes until the pastry is golden brown.

RATATOUILLE

This simple ratatouille is perfect for pizza toppings or for filling tarts and gougères.

SERVES 4-6

4-5 tablespoons olive oil
1 large onion, chopped
2-3 plump cloves garlic, chopped
1 medium aubergine, cut into 2.5 cm (1 inch) cubes
1 red and 1 green pepper, cut into 2.5 cm (1 inch) pieces
4-6 large tomatoes, peeled and diced
sea salt and black pepper
1 tablespoon fresh thyme leaves
3-4 medium courgettes, diced

Heat the oil in a large heavy bottomed pan and cook the onion for 3-4 minutes, until soft but not brown. Stir in the garlic and cook for a further minute. Now put in the aubergine, peppers and tomatoes. Stir well, add salt and pepper and the thyme.

Bring to the boil and simmer over a gentle heat for 25-30 minutes. Stir in the courgettes and cook the ratatouille for a further 5-7 minutes. Taste and correct the seasoning.

PISSALADIÈRE

This bread-based onion tart comes from the South of France. It is both delicious and filling.

SERVES 6-8

340 g (12 oz) strong white bread flour
1 teaspoon salt
1 sachet easy-blend yeast
1 tablespoon olive oil
about 175 ml (6 fl oz) warm water

FOR THE TOPPING
3 large red or white skinned onions, thinly sliced
3 tablespoons olive oil
1 tin anchovies in oil
115 g (4 oz) stoned black olives, halved
black pepper

Mix the flour, salt and yeast together and add the oil. Use enough water to make a soft but workable dough and knead for about 5 minutes or until smooth. Allow to rise for about 1 hour or until doubled in size, then punch down, knead lightly and roll or stretch to fit your largest baking sheet.

Meanwhile, cook the onions over a low heat in the oil for 40-50 minutes until very soft. Spread them over the dough. Cut the anchovies into fine strips and lay them in lattice fashion on top of the onions. Place half an olive in each diamond and grind over some black pepper.

Bake the pissaladière in a preheated oven at 200°C/400°F/Gas 6 for 30 minutes or until the dough is well risen and cooked through.

RATATOUILLE PIZZA WITH A WHOLEMEAL CRUST

SERVES 4-6

450 g (1 lb) wholemeal flour
1 sachet easy-blend yeast
1 teaspoon salt
2 tablespoons oil
scant 275 ml (½ pint) warm water

FOR THE TOPPING
1 batch ratatouille (see page 149)
225 g (8 oz) feta cheese
fresh thyme or oregano leaves
1 tablespoon chilli oil or virgin olive oil
sea salt and black pepper

Make the base in the usual way, mixing the flour, yeast and salt then adding the oil and water to give a soft but workable dough. Knead for 5-10 minutes, cover, then leave to double in size. Knock back the dough and divide into 2 pieces. Roll or pull each piece into a 20 cm (8 inch) circle and place on baking sheets. Leave for 15 minutes.

Divide the ratatouille between the pizzas, then crumble on the feta cheese. Scatter on some thyme or oregano leaves, then drizzle over the oil and season. Bake in a preheated oven at 220°C/425°F/Gas 7 until the dough is crisp and the cheese golden brown.

RATATOUILLE-FILLLED GOUGÈRE

Gougères are baked choux pastry rings that can be stuffed with any number of delicious fillings. Here I have chosen that wonderful summer dish ratatouille (see page 149).

SERVES 4

1 quantity ratatouille (see page 149)

FOR THE CHOUX PASTRY
**70 g (2½ oz) plain flour
pinch of salt
140 ml (¼ pint) water
60 g (2 oz) butter
2 size 3 eggs
1 tablespoon chopped chives
1 tablespoon chopped parsley
1 teaspoon mild mustard
85 g (3 oz) cubed Emmenthal cheese or Cheddar cheese**

Sift the flour and salt together. Do not leave out this important step.

Put the water and butter in a heavy bottomed pan over a low heat. Warm until the butter has melted then turn up the heat and bring to a full rolling boil. Add the flour, all at once, then remove from the heat, beating frantically with a wooden spoon.

The mixture should form a smooth soft ball and come completely away from the sides of the pan. If the mixture is wet and sticks to the pan cook over a medium heat, still beating, for a few minutes.

Allow the dough to cool, then beat in the eggs, one at a time. The finished paste should be glossy and stiff enough to hold soft peaks. You may not need all the last egg.

Fold in the herbs, mustard and cheese cubes and spoon the paste around the edge of a well-greased round or oval ovenproof dish.

Bake the gougère in a preheated oven at 220°C/425°F/Gas 7 for 10 minutes, then turn down the heat to 180°C/360°F/Gas 4 and cook for a further 20-25 minutes.

Meanwhile heat the ratatouille and when the gougère is cooked, spoon this into the centre and serve at once.

Cheese & Eggs

This chapter on cheese and eggs is not just for vegetarians. When I cook for non meat-eaters I like to serve dishes that are so delicious they rate inclusion in the meal on their own merits.

I am a passionate fan of cheese, especially cheeses from the small British creameries. I hope EEC regulations will continue to allow them to grow and flourish, increasing choice and rebuilding what was for years a sadly declining industry.

I must mention a few of my favourite cheeses. We now have a blue sheeps milk cheese, Beenleigh Blue, to rival the finest Rocquefort. It comes from Robin Congden of Totnes, Devon, who also produces the goats milk cheese Harbourne Blue. Both are wonderful examples of the cheesemaker's craft. Then there is Bonchester, a rich golden Camembert-style cheese, made from Jersey milk, by the Curtis family at Hawick on the Scottish borders. There are also splendid English Cheddars, Double Gloucesters, Cheshires and Caerphilly cheeses being made all over the country in small owner-run dairies, and I would urge anyone visiting London to sample them at the Neal's Yard Dairy, 17 Shorts Garden WC2. The shop is run by Randolph Hodgson and his well informed staff, who will be only too happy to help you find exactly what you're looking for.

When you break an egg that's really fresh, it will sit pertly in the pan, with the yolk standing proud. New-laid eggs take slightly longer to boil than those that have been in the larder for a few days.

The grandest looking egg dish is the soufflé. It is, in fact, quite simple to make, and can even be cooked ahead and reheated, when it will be slightly heavier, but no less delicious. Almost any flavouring – meat, fish, cheese or herbs – can be used in a soufflé, as long as the pieces are not so heavy that they sink to the bottom of the dish. Use the basic mixture and method and experiment with your own flavourings.

WELSH RAREBIT

I often simply melt a slice of mature Cheddar on a slice of granary toast, but when I'm looking for a more sophisticated flavour I make this quick cheese sauce.

MAKES 2-3 ROUNDS

115 g (4 oz) mature Cheddar, grated
1 tablespoon butter
3-4 tablespoons beer
1 tablespoon mild mustard
hot buttered toast

Place all the ingredients in a nonstick pan and warm over a low heat. Stir the mixture until piping hot and well combined. Spoon on to toast and brown under a hot grill.

AVOCADO AND PARMESAN FOCACCIA

This is one of my favourite simple summer lunch dishes. The combination of flavours is delicious and the colours are a delight.

SERVES 4

2 ripe avocados
4 thick slices focaccia (rich olive oil bread)
about 115 g (4 oz) piece parmesan cheese
8 anchovy fillets
salad leaves
olive oil and wine vinegar dressing
black pepper

Peel, stone and slice the avocados. Place a slice of focaccia on each plate and arrange the avocado slices on top. Flake the cheese on top of the avocado.

Lay 2 fillets of anchovy in a diagonal cross over the cheese, arrange a few salad leaves on the plates, then drizzle a little oil and vinegar over both the leaves and the sandwich. Season with freshly ground black pepper; you will not need salt as the anchovies and parmesan are both quite salty.

CRUSTED CAERPHILLY AND LEEK BAKE

*A good recipe for early summer when leeks are still in the shops, this lovely creamy
dish can also be made with celery hearts.*

SERVES 4

900 g (2 lb) leeks
45 g (1½ oz) butter
45 g (1½ oz) flour
600 ml (1 pint) creamy milk
salt and pepper
1 teaspoon mustard powder
115 g (4 oz) crumbled Caerphilly cheese

FOR THE TOPPING
85 g (3 oz) crumbled Caerphilly cheese
85 g (3 oz) fresh brown breadcrumbs
½ teaspoon celery salt
1 tablespoon chopped parsley

TO FINISH
2 tablespoons melted butter

Reserve the green leek tops for another occasion, and cut the white part of
the leeks into 2.5 cm (1 inch) pieces. Blanch the prepared leeks in boiling
water for 2 minutes, drain well and arrange in a buttered ovenproof dish.

Make a cheese sauce by melting the butter with the flour and beating
in the milk. Simmer for 3-4 minutes, then season and stir in the mustard
powder and cheese. Pour the sauce over the leeks.

In a food processor whizz together the topping ingredients and
sprinkle in an even layer over the sauce. Drizzle on the butter and bake in
a hot oven at 180°C/360°F/Gas 4 for 30-40 minutes.

LEEK AND CAERPHILLY FILO BUNDLES

These pretty bundles could also be filled with Cheddar cheese and courgettes.

SERVES 4

3 medium leeks
salt and black pepper
4 x 30 x 42.5 cm (12 x 18 inch) sheets filo pastry
30 g (1 oz) butter, melted
170 g (6 oz) Caerphilly cheese, crumbled
1-2 teaspoons sesame seeds

Clean the leeks and slice into strips about 10 cm (4 inches) long. Blanch in plenty of boiling salted water for 60 seconds, then drain well.

Brush a sheet of filo with melted butter and fold in half to form a chunky shape. Place a quarter of the leeks and a quarter of the crumbled cheese in the centre of the sheet and season with a little black pepper. Gather up the sheet and press the pastry together to form a bundle with a ragged top. Make sure the cheese and leeks are sealed inside the bundle. Continue until you have 4 bundles.

Place the bundles on a baking sheet and brush with the remaining butter. Sprinkle with sesame seeds and bake in a preheated oven at 200°C/400°F/Gas 6 for 15-20 minutes until golden brown. Serve with a dressed green salad.

GLAMORGAN 'SAUSAGES'

*This recipe came to me from Franco Taruschio who is the proprietor of the
Walnut Tree Inn, Abergavenny. These traditional Welsh cheese croquettes have
proved very popular with everyone who has tried them. They travel well and
so make excellent picnic food.*

SERVES 4

**225 g (8 oz) Caerphilly cheese
170 g (6 oz) white day-old breadcrumbs
3 tablespoons chopped spring onions
2 tablespoons chopped parsley
3 size 3 eggs**

TO FINISH
**flour, egg and breadcrumbs
oil for frying**

Put all the ingredients for the 'sausages' into the bowl of a food processor
and process until everything is finely chopped and the mixture begins to
form a ball.

Turn it out on to a board, pinch off small balls, and roll into sausages
about 7.5 cm (3 inches) long. When all the mixture is shaped, roll the
sausages in flour then dip in beaten egg and coat with breadcrumbs. Chill
for about 30 minutes.

Shallow-fry the sausages over a medium heat until golden brown on
all sides. Drain on absorbent paper and serve with salad.

COURGETTE AND CHEESE BAKE

The inspiration for this recipe came after a visit to my uncle's bountiful garden in Chesham Bois. John proudly lifted back the leaves of his courgette plants to show that in only one short day, another seven courgettes were ready for harvest.

SERVES 4

1 medium onion, chopped
1 tablespoon butter
1 clove garlic, crushed and chopped
450 g (1 lb) firm young courgettes
275 ml (½ pint) milk
2 size 2 eggs, beaten
225 g (8 oz) cottage cheese, sieved
115 g (4 oz) mature Cheddar cheese, grated
1 teaspoon chopped fresh thyme
1 teaspoon Dijon mustard
170 g (6 oz) day-old wholemeal breadcrumbs
salt and black pepper

Fry the onion in the butter until soft, add the garlic and cook for a further 60 seconds.

Finely grate the courgettes and add them to the pan. Turn up the heat and cook for 3-4 minutes, tossing the courgettes so that most of the liquid is cooked off.

Mix the courgettes and all the remaining ingredients together, season to taste and pour into a greased ovenproof dish. Bake in a preheated oven at 190°C/375°F/Gas 5 for 45 mintues. Serve hot or warm.

COURGETTE, DILL AND FROMAGE FRAIS MOUSSE

This is a delicate gelatine-set mousse, perfect cool food for a hot summer's evening. Serve hot herb bread to give crunch and contrast. Instead of the cold tomato coulis you can use my fresh tomato sauce recipe on page 88, cold.

SERVES 4

3 tablespoons water
1½ teaspoons powdered gelatine
225 g (8 oz) firm courgettes
salt and pepper
225 g (8 oz) 8% fromage frais
3 tablespoons chopped fresh dill
wine vinegar
275ml (½ pint) cold tomato coulis
Tabasco
fresh dill fronds

Put the water in a small bowl and sprinkle on the gelatine. Leave to swell.

Grate the courgettes into a colander and sprinkle with salt. Leave for 30 minutes, then rinse well under cold running water and squeeze dry. Press the mass of courgettes with a paper towel to extract as much moisture as possible.

Stir the fromage frais until smooth, then stir in the courgettes. Add the dill and season to taste; you may not need any more salt. Add a few drops of wine vinegar to sharpen the flavour. Stir the dissolved gelatine into the courgette mixture. Divide between 4 ramekin dishes and put into the fridge to set.

Run a sharp knife round each mousse and turn on to individual plates. Season the tomato coulis with Tabasco, spoon a little around each mousse and garnish with a frond or two of fresh dill.

These mousses are delicious served with fresh prawns.

CHEESE, EGG AND SUN-DRIED TOMATO BRUNCH BAKE

This dish is good for a light lunch or supper, but I usually serve it on a warm summer's day, for brunch in the garden. With yoghurt, fresh rolls, coffee and perhaps some champagne, it makes a wonderful treat.

This recipe is best when assembled the day before it is needed and refrigerated overnight.

SERVES 6

**4 medium slices two-day-old bread
115 g (4 oz) grated Cheddar cheese
4-6 sun-dried tomato halves, chopped
415 ml (¾ pint) milk
4 size 2 eggs, beaten
½ teaspoon mild mustard
salt and pepper**

Cut the bread into 2.5 cm (1 inch) squares and place in a well-greased ovenproof dish. Sprinkle over the cheese and scatter on the tomato pieces. Beat the remaining ingredients together and pour over. Place in the fridge for at least 1 hour, but preferably overnight.

Heat the oven to 180°C/360°F/Gas 4 and bake for 30-40 minutes until puffy and golden. Serve hot.

FRESH HERB OMELETTE

One of the delights of early summer is this combination of freshly picked young herbs full of bright green flavour, free-range eggs and butter. Serve with the very best bread you can find or make your own, and you have a meal fit for angels.

SERVES 1

**2-3 size 2 free-range eggs
1 tablespoon each chopped fresh parsley, tarragon and chives
sea salt and black pepper
butter**

Whisk the eggs with a dash of cold water, the herbs and salt and pepper to taste.

Heat your omelette pan well. Add a walnut-sized lump of butter and swirl it around the pan as it melts. Still swirling, pour in the egg and return the pan to the heat. Cook over a very high heat, moving the edges of the cooked egg into the centre with a fork or spatula, and allowing the raw egg to run to the outside. Continue until the omelette is cooked to your liking, then tip from the pan, folding it on to a plate. Serve at once.

SALMON AND TARRAGON SOUFFLÉ

SERVES 4

1 tablespoon dry breadcrumbs
60 g (2 oz) freshly grated parmesan cheese
45 g (1½ oz) butter
45 g (1½ oz) flour
275 ml (½ pint) milk
sea salt and white pepper
4 egg yolks
170 g (6 oz) cooked salmon, flaked
1 tablespoon chopped fresh tarragon
4-6 egg whites

Heat the oven to 200°C/400°F/Gas 6.

Butter an 18 cm (7 inch) soufflé dish well and dust the inside with the breadcrumbs mixed with about half a tablespoon of the parmesan cheese.

Make a thick white sauce with the butter, flour and milk. Simmer for 2-3 minutes to cook the sauce, then season and stir in the cheese. Allow to cool for a few minutes and then beat in the egg yolks one at a time. Fold in the salmon and the tarragon.

Put the egg whites in a large bowl and whisk until stiff but not dry. If you overwhisk it will be difficult to fold the whites in successfully, so stop as soon as they hold their shape and will not fall from the bowl when you turn it upside down.

Beat one spoonful of egg white into the salmon mixture to soften it, then carefully cut and fold the salmon mixture into the whites. Pour into the soufflé dish and bake in the heated oven for 25-30 minutes until well risen and golden brown.

A well cooked soufflé should still be slightly runny inside. Serve at once.

If you want to cook ahead use four 10 cm (4 inch) dishes. Cook the soufflés for 15-20 minutes and turn from the dishes when cold. Put the cooked soufflés in an ovenproof dish and cover with film until needed.

To reheat, pour over about 140 ml (¼ pint) single cream and cook in a preheated oven at 180C°/360°F/Gas 4 for 10-15 minutes. Serve scattered with a little fresh tarragon.

CHEESE AND COURGETTE SOUFFLÉ

SERVES 4

1 tablespoon breadcrumbs mixed with ½ tablespoon grated parmesan cheese
450 g (1 lb) firm young courgettes
freshly grated nutmeg, sea salt and black pepper
70 g (2½ oz) butter
45 g (1½ oz) flour
275 ml (½ pint milk)
115 g (4 oz) mature Cheddar cheese, grated
4 size 2 egg yolks
4-6 egg whites

Butter an 18 cm (7 inch) soufflé dish and coat the inside with the cheese and breadcrumb mixture. Heat the oven to 200°C/400°F/Gas 6.

Grate the courgettes coarsely into a colander, sprinkle with salt and leave for 30 minutes. Rinse under running cold water, then squeeze as dry as possible. Heat 30 g (1 oz) butter in a frying pan and cook the courgettes over a high heat for 1-2 minutes. Allow to cool.

Make a white sauce using the remaining butter, flour and milk. Simmer for 2-3 minutes to cook the flour. Stir in the cheese and season with salt, pepper and nutmeg. Add the egg yolks one at a time, then fold in the courgettes.

Whisk the egg whites in a large bowl until stiff, then mix one tablespoon of the whites into the cheese mixture. Pour the cheese mixture into the remaining whites and carefully fold together. Pour into the prepared dish and bake in the hot oven for 25-30 minutes.

This soufflé is not suitable for baking ahead.

STUFFED EGGS

These eggs, filled with a tasty mixture of fish and capers, are often served in Spanish tapas bars.

SERVES 4

6 hardboiled eggs
about 225 g (8 oz) tuna fish, flaked
5-6 tablespoons mayonnaise
1 teaspoon finely chopped capers
salt and pepper

TO FINISH
paprika
1 tablespoon chopped parsley

Slice the eggs in half and scoop out the yolks. Put these into a bowl and mash in the remaining ingredients. Season to taste.

Stuff the mixture back into the whites and arrange on a serving dish. Sprinkle with a little paprika and scatter over the parsley.

EGG SALAD WITH SAFFRON MAYONNAISE

A pretty dish with the rich fragrant flavour of saffron, this looks lovely served on a bed of dark green frisée lettuce.

SERVES 4

1 pinch saffron strands
2 tablespoons white wine vinegar
2 raw egg yolks
scant teaspoon Dijon mustard
175 ml (6 fl oz) light olive oil
sea salt and black pepper
6 hardboiled eggs
frisée lettuce

Heat the saffron strands in a long handled metal spoon, and when they begin to roast, crush to a powder with the back of another spoon. Put the powder into the wine vinegar and leave to soak for 20 minutes.

Put the yolks, half the vinegar and the mustard in a food processor and whizz until smooth. With the motor running, add the oil in a very fine stream. Pour in the remaining vinegar, then taste and correct the seasoning.

Cut the eggs in half and place on a bed of frisée lettuce. Spoon a little mayonnaise over each egg and serve.

PESTO AND TOMATO ROULADE

All the delicious flavour of pesto in a meltingly tender roulade: this is like eating air. It really is easy to make, so don't be put off by the lengthy instructions.

SERVES 6

2 tablespoons freshly grated parmesan cheese
30 g (1 oz) butter
30 g (1 oz) plain flour
275 ml (½ pint) milk
generous tablespoon pesto (see page 87)
3 size 2 egg yolks
salt and pepper
4 size 2 egg whites
4-6 ripe tomatoes
1-2 tablespoons milk
170 g (6 oz) garlic and herb flavoured soft cheese

TO FINISH
1 tablespoon each chopped parsley and parmesan cheese

Grease a swiss roll tin well and line it with greaseproof paper, folded up to make 2.5 cm (1 inch) high sides. Brush this with butter and sprinkle on about half the parmesan cheese.

Melt the butter in a heavy pan and add the flour. Mix well, then add the milk, stirring to give a smooth white sauce. Simmer for 3-4 minutes. Allow to cool.

Add the pesto, then beat in the egg yolks one at a time. Season with salt and pepper. Whisk the egg whites and then fold the pesto mixture into them with a metal spoon. Pour into the prepared tin.

Bake the roulade in a preheated oven at 200°C/400°F/Gas 6 for 15-20 minutes, until well risen and golden brown.

Prepare a sheet of greaseproof paper large enough to take the roulade and scatter on the remaining parmesan cheese. Take the roulade out of the oven and turn it on to the prepared paper. Cover with a damp cloth and allow to cool completely.

Place the tomatoes in a bowl and cover with boiling water for 2-3 minutes. Peel off the skins. Discard the seeds and dice the flesh. Beat the milk into the cheese to a soft spreading consistency.

Once the roulade is cool, peel off the paper and spread on the cheese. Scatter over the diced tomatoes and roll up the roulade carefully. Don't worry if it cracks slightly. Carefully transfer it to a serving dish and scatter on the chopped parsley and parmesan cheese.

WATERCRESS PANCAKES FILLED WITH MUSHROOMS

The idea for these pancakes comes from Stephen Ross, one-time owner of the Homewood Park Hotel and now owner of the Queensbury Hotel in Bath. For preference, I use a ragoût of wild and cultivated mushrooms napped with cream, which contrasts well with the sharp green flavour of the crêpes.

SERVES 4-6

115 g (4 oz) plain flour
2 size 2 eggs
30 g (1 oz) melted butter
salt and pepper
60 g (2 oz) dark green watercress leaves

FOR THE FILLING
45 g (1½ oz) butter
340 g (12 oz) mixed wild and cultivated mushrooms (cleaned weight), roughly chopped
1 clove garlic, crushed and chopped
1 tablespoon dry sherry
1 tablespoon flour
200 ml (⅓ pint) single cream
salt and pepper
1 tablespoon chopped parsley

TO FINISH
2 tablespoons freshly grated parmesan cheese

First make the batter. Combine all the ingredients in a blender and process until the watercress is finely chopped and the mixture is smooth and green.

Now make very thin crêpes, layering them with greaseproof paper as they are ready. Keep 12 pancakes to one side; wrap and freeze the remainder for another day.

Melt the butter in a saucepan and when it is hot put in the mushrooms and toss over a high heat for 3-4 minutes. Add the garlic and cook for a further 60 seconds. Now pour on the sherry and stir, cooking until the liquid evaporates. Sprinkle on the flour, mix in well and then add the cream, stirring to give a smooth sauce. If the sauce seems very thick add a little milk. Simmer for 2-3 minutes or until no taste of raw flour remains, then season to taste and stir in the parsley.

Top each crêpe with a generous spoonful of the filling. Folding them into triangles, place in a buttered ovenproof dish, and reheat in a hot oven at 200°C/400°F/Gas 6 for 10-15 minutes. Serve sprinkled with parmesan.

SUMMER PUDDINGS & DESSERTS

It's hard to know where to start when introducing a chapter on what is one of the most wonderful aspects of summer eating. Sitting stuffed to the point of collapse in a strawberry field, carefully negotiating the thorns when picking ripened gooseberries, or sneaking raspberries from the punnet on the way home from the shops, the delights of summer fruits are many.

No one needs to eat puddings to survive, but I would strongly argue that our emotional and spirtual welfare is much enhanced by something as delicious as a bowl of Summer pudding topped with thick Jersey cream.

For this chapter, I have chosen the recipes that are best loved by my family. Angel food cake is a popular birthday treat, summer fruit brûlée an all-time favourite and elderflower sorbet, made at the very start of the summer, a promise of good things to come.

The relaxed style of summer eating lends itself to all sorts of satisfyingly creamy and fruity desserts, mousses and perhaps my favourite of all – homemade ice cream.

At its simplest form good ice cream can be made by lightly whipping double cream, folding in sugar and fruit purée, and freezing. The high fat content of double cream gives a reasonable texture and the mixture does not need beating while it freezes.

Custard-style ice creams are the most common and, to my mind, the best in both taste and texture. Egg yolks are cooked with cream or milk and the resulting custard is flavoured, cooled and then churned until frozen. Without an electric ice cream churn, you will have to beat a custard ice several times while it freezes to ensure a smooth, light texture. Ice cream made with egg yolks should be eaten within one week of making, as the yolks are not thoroughly cooked. The product should be treated as if it were fresh.

Parfait ices guarantee a good result each time. These are made by whipping eggs and sugar syrup to a mousse, then folding in whipped cream. The resulting airy mass is frozen without churning.

Parfaits have a wonderfully light texture and make impressive dinner party desserts.

Sorbets are deliciously refreshing and can be made in a great variety of different flavours. Fruit sorbets based on sugar syrup make lovely puddings, while Champagne or fancy tea sorbets add a touch of elegance to any meal. Savoury sorbets make an unusual refreshing course on a hot day.

I asked Shaun Hill, Gidleigh Park's much lauded chef, for any tips he might have on how to make the perfect ice cream and he said one should never underestimate the importance of alcohol. He explained that it acts as an antifreeze to soften the ice, a useful ingredient for the cook who has forgotten to take the mixture from the freezer those vital 20 minutes before serving. Shaun recommends 1 tablespoon spirit per 600 ml (1 pint) of custard. He stresses the importance of tasting the mixture before freezing and adjusting the flavours at that point, bearing in mind that freezing dulls flavour.

The usual recipe for a custard ice is 4 egg yolks to 600 ml (1 pint) of single cream, with sugar added to taste depending on the other flavours used. Strained fruit purée is stirred into the cold custard; melted chocolate into the warm mixture. Always chill the mixture before you begin freezing. If you have an electric ice cream churn, the custard ice is the best. Don't use double cream in an electric churn, as the mixture will whip before it freezes – with disastrous result.

I use a simple electric churn at home, the bowl of which has to be pre-frozen in the freezer. It makes about 900 ml (1½ pints) ice cream, is inexpensive to buy and takes up very little storage space. The main disadvantage is that the bowl needs about 10 hours in the freezer between batches, so planning is necessary. You could buy a spare bowl if you have the space and store both bowls frozen ready for use, but as homemade ice cream is a treat I would always serve bought ice cream if catering for large numbers.

For serious ice cream lovers there are large machines with built-in freezing units. I have tried the Gelato Chef 2000, which is easy to use and has a quiet motor. It produces wonderfully smooth ice cream without any forward planning – a hedonist's delight!

SUMMER PUDDING

I always had a problem with this classic pudding until I started making it with brown instead of white bread. The flavour of the pudding is unaltered but the texture is much superior.

SERVES 4-6

675 g (1½ lb) assorted summer fruits
6-8 slices wholemeal bread
115 g (4 oz) caster sugar or to taste

Wash the fruit and remove any leaves or stems. Put the most robust berries in a pan with some sugar. Warm until the juice runs, then simmer, adding the fruit in order of tenderness. Black and red currants should go in first and raspberries or sliced strawberries can be stirred in once the pan has been removed from the heat.

Cut the crusts from the bread and press them into a 600 ml (1 pint) pudding basin, lining it as neatly as possible. Spoon in the fruit and enough juice to fill the bowl. Reserve any remaining juice.

Cut the remaining slices of bread to form a lid and press the joins together well. Put a small plate on top of the pudding, weight it and refrigerate overnight.

To serve the pudding, remove the plate and if necessary carefully run a palette knife around the outside of the pudding to free it from the bowl. Invert on to a plate, spoon over any reserved juices and serve with cream as soon as possible after it has been turned out.

SIMPLE SUMMER PUDDINGS

This is a cheat's recipe but so good and so easy that no one will complain.

SERVES 4

generous 450 g (1 lb) assorted summer berries
caster sugar to taste
1 tablespoon crème de cassis
4 x 2-day old brioche buns

Wash and trim the berries and place in a large saucepan with a little sugar. Warm and mash lightly until the berries have yielded their juice. Cook for 2-3 minutes, add the crème de cassis and extra sugar if needed, then allow to cool.

Meanwhile, slice the tops from the brioche rolls and carefully scrape out hollows inside. Discard the crumbs or use in another recipe.

Spoon the berrries into the brioche cases and put on the lids. Reserve any extra fruit or juice.

Refrigerate overnight then serve with cream and any extra fruit.

JUMBLEBERRY PIE

If you ever have a mixture of berries, some over-ripe, others a little green, this is a recipe for you. I often make this pie after a visit to the pick-your-own farm where I always overbuy, finding the long fields of berries so tempting.

SERVES 4-6

285 g (10 oz) ready made shortcrust pastry
900 g (2 lb) mixed berries, washed and trimmed
2 level tablespoons plain flour
1 teaspoon cinnamon
4 tablespoons caster sugar
250 g (9 oz) ready made puff pastry
beaten egg and sugar to glaze

Roll out the shortcrust pastry and use it to line a shallow 22.5 cm (9 inch) pie dish. Pile in the berries. Mix together the flour, cinnamon and sugar and scatter this over the fruit.

Roll out the puff pastry to form a lid and place it on the pie, pressing edges well to seal. Cut an air vent in the centre and glaze the pie with beaten egg and sugar.

Bake in a preheated oven at 200°C/400°F/Gas 6 for 30-40 minutes or until the pastry is cooked and a rich golden brown.

Serve warm with double cream.

TAYBERRY TURNOVERS

These long vermilion berries are a cross between a raspberry and a blackberry.
Although sweet when very ripe they are quite tart if picked a little early. They stand up
to cooking well, producing lots of lovely red juice.

SERVES 6

225 g (8 oz) ready made puff pastry
1 size 2 egg, separated
2 tablespoons caster sugar
60 g (2 oz) mascarpone or cream cheese
225 g (8 oz) tayberries
sugar to glaze

Roll out the pastry and cut 6 x 10 cm (4 inch) circles. Beat the egg yolk
with the sugar and cream cheese. Place a spoonful of the cheese mixture
on each pastry circle. Divide the berries between the circles. Dampen the
edges of the pastry and fold over to enclose the filling. Press to seal. Place
the turnovers on a baking sheet.

Whisk the egg white and brush the pastry with this to glaze. Sprinkle
with sugar and bake in a preheated oven at 200°C/400°F/Gas 6 for about
20 minutes or until puffy and golden brown. Serve hot with cream.

BLACKCURRANT STIRABOUT

*This is a very pretty dessert. As blackcurrants are time-consuming to top and tail, I
wash them well then sieve out all the stems, skins and pips.*

SERVES 4-6

340 g (12 oz) blackcurrants
sugar to taste
1 teaspoon arrowroot
275 ml (½ pint) double cream
275 ml (½ pint) natural Greek yoghurt
4 amaretti biscuits, crumbled

Put the prepared fruit in a saucepan with 140 ml (¼ pint) water.
Heat slowly until the juice flows, then simmer for 2-3 minutes, adding
sugar to taste.

Rub the contents of the pan through a fine sieve then return the purée
to a clean pan and add the arrowroot, slaked with 1 tablespoon of water.
Bring to the boil, stirring constantly, then simmer for 2 minutes until thick
and glossy. Allow to cool.

Whip the cream until it thickens, then beat in the yoghurt.

Put a layer of cream in a glass serving dish, cover it with half the fruit
purée, then sprinkle on the crumbs. Now add another layer of cream and
another of fruit. Take a long skewer or fine bladed knife and stir the layers
carefully, just enough to create swirls.

Chill and serve cold.

Raspberry chiffon pie

This is a light airy pie filled with a fruit flavoured mousse. I developed such a passion for chiffon pies when I lived in New Jersey that I had to take detours around the bakery store to stop myself from buying too many.

SERVES 4-6

22.5 cm (9 inch) shortcrust pie shell baked blind

FOR THE FILLING
450 g (1 lb) raspberries
1 sachet gelatine
115 g (4 oz) caster sugar
275 ml (½ pint) double cream
4 egg whites

Purée the raspberries and rub through a sieve to remove the pips.

Sprinkle the gelatine over 3 tablespoons water and allow to swell. Once it has absorbed all the water, warm the bowl until the mixture is clear and liquid. Add this to the raspberry purée along with half the sugar. Beat the cream until it holds soft peaks.

In a clean bowl, whisk the egg whites with spotlessly clean beaters until they thicken. Whisk in the remaining sugar and continue beating until you have a stiff glossy mixture.

Once the raspberry purée is on the point of setting, fold in the cream and then the meringue. Pour into the cold pie shell and chill for 1-2 hours. Decorate with berries or small edible flowers.

ANGEL FOOD CAKE WITH FRESH BERRIES

Angel food cake is feather light and white as snow. It makes a beautiful birthday cake topped with berries for a summer party and has the added advantage of using all the egg white you have left from making mayonnaise.

You will need a ring mould tin about 25 cm (10 inches) in diameter. I use a large springform tin with a ring mould insert. All your utensils must be grease-free.

SERVES 4-6

70 g (2½ oz) plain flour
115 g (4 oz) icing sugar
scant teaspoon cream of tartar
pinch of salt
6 egg whites
85 g (3 oz) caster sugar
1½ teaspoons vanilla essence
¼ teaspoon almond essence

Sift the flour with the icing sugar 3 times.

Put the cream of tartar, salt and egg whites in the bowl of a free-standing electric mixer and beat until frothy. Whisk the mixture on high speed, adding the caster sugar a little at a time until you have a very stiff glossy meringue. Carefully fold the icing sugar/flour mixture and the two essences into the egg whites with a metal spoon.

Spoon the mixture into the ungreased cake tin and cut through the mixture two or three times with a sharp knife to break up any large air bubbles. Bake in a preheated oven at 180°C/360°F/Gas 4 for 30-35 minutes, or until the cake is golden brown and the top springs back when lightly touched.

Take the tin out of the oven and invert it over a bottle, so it hangs upside down with the top of the cake exposed. After two hours, slip a palette knife around the edges of the cake, give the tin a sharp tap, and turn the cake out on to a serving dish.

Serve with whipped cream and fresh fruit.

Apples baked in elderflower syrup

This is a good way to use the highly scented elderflowers found in the hedgerows in early summer.

Serves 4

225 g (8 oz) caster sugar
600 ml (1 pint) water
a handful elderflower heads
4 Golden Delicious, peeled and cored

Make a sugar syrup by dissolving the sugar in the water and simmering for about 5 minutes. Infuse the elderflower heads in the syrup for 30 minutes, then remove. Cut the apples in half, make deep cuts almost all the way through, and place core side down in a baking dish.

Pour over the syrup and bake in a preheated oven at 180°C/360°F/ Gas 4 for 20-25 minutes. Serve warm with soured cream.

Lemon cream tart

Serves 4-6

225 g (8 oz) sweet shortcrust pastry
finely grated zest and juice of 2 large lemons
85 g (3 oz) caster sugar
60 g (2 oz) butter
3 size 2 eggs
275 ml (½ pint) double cream

Roll out the pastry as thinly as possible and use to line a 22 cm (8 inch) flan tin. Cover with paper and baking beans and bake in a preheated oven at 200°C/400°F/Gas 6 for 10 minutes. Remove the paper and beans and continue to cook the pastry case until it is lightly browned. Remove from the oven and allow to cool on a rack, then remove from the tin.

Put the lemon zest and juice, sugar and butter in a heavy bottomed saucepan. Heat until the butter has melted and the sugar dissolved. Remove from the heat and allow to cool for a moment. Whisk the eggs together and add to the mixture.

Return the mixture to the heat, whisking constantly, and cook until the curd thickens. When the first bubble breaks on the surface, remove from the heat at once. By this time the mixture should be very thick. Whisk from time to time while the curd cools.

Whisk the cream until it holds soft peaks, then whisk in the curd. Spoon this mixture into the pie shell not more than 1 hour before serving.

FRENCH APRICOT TART

This recipe is made in seconds from easily assembled ingredients and ready-made puff pastry.

SERVES 4-6

225 g (8 oz) ready-made puff pastry
about 8 large apricots, halved and stoned
2 size 2 eggs, beaten
200 ml (⅓ pint) crème fraîche
2 tablespoons caster sugar
1 teaspoon vanilla essence
about 1 tablespoon extra sugar

Roll out the pastry to fill a shallow 22 cm (8 inch) flan tin. Lay the apricots face down on the pastry.

Beat together the eggs, crème fraîche, sugar and vanilla, then pour over the fruit. Sprinkle the top with a little extra sugar and bake in a preheated oven at 220°C/425°F/Gas 7 for 25-30 minutes.

The pastry should be cooked and the top of the tart a dark golden brown. Sometimes the edges of the fruit are slightly charred, which is how it is served in France.

BANANA PARCELS

These parcels can be cooked on a barbecue. They sit quite happily on the grill over the last heat from the coals and can be prepared by even the youngest chefs. Almost any combination of fruit can be used, but with berries I might use white sugar and perhaps some crème de cassis.

SERVES 6

6 medium bananas
2 tablespoons butter
2-3 tablespoons soft brown sugar
4 tablespoons double cream
2 tablespoons rum (optional)

Cut 6 large squares of foil. Peel and slice the bananas and divide between the foil squares. Now divide the remaining ingredients between the parcels.

Gather up the foil, twisting the top to seal, and either place on a cooling barbecue grill for 20 minutes or put on a baking sheet in a preheated oven at 190°C/375°F/Gas 5 for about 20 mintues.

Serve with vanilla ice cream.

Fresh fig cake

SERVES 4-6

60 g (2 oz) butter
4 size 3 eggs
125 g (4½ oz) caster sugar
125 g (4½ oz) plain flour

FOR THE SYRUP
60 g (2 oz) caster sugar
140 ml (¼ pint) water
2-3 tablespoons orange liqueur
6 fresh figs
3 tablespoons redcurrant jelly

Melt the butter and allow to cool. Put the eggs and sugar in the bowl of a free-standing mixer and beat on high speed for 10 minutes until you have a very dense foam that forms a thick ribbon when the beaters are lifted from the bowl.

Sift the flour and fold into the mousse one third at a time. Fold in the melted butter with the last batch of flour. Spoon the mixture into a greased, floured 22 cm (8 inch) sponge tin and bake in the centre of a preheated oven at 180°C/360°F/Gas 4 for 35-40 minutes, or until the cake is golden brown and shrinks slightly from the sides of the tin.

Remove from the oven and allow the cake to cool in the tin for 15 minutes. Remove the cake and finish cooling on a rack.

For the syrup, put the sugar and water in a saucepan and heat until the sugar has dissolved. Bring to the boil and simmer for 5 minutes. Cool and add the liqueur.

Place the cake on a serving dish and spoon the liqueur-flavoured syrup over the top. Peel and slice the figs and arrange the slices on the cake. Melt the redcurrant jelly with 2 teaspoons water, stirring until smooth. Allow to cool a little, then brush over the fruit to glaze.

Serve with cream or crème fraîche.

Buttered pear pudding with calvados sauce

Serves 4-6

675 g (1½ lb) firm ripe pears, peeled and cored
45 g (1½ oz) butter
juice of ½ lemon

For the sponge
115 g (4 oz) butter
115 g (4 oz) caster sugar
115 g (4 oz) self-raising flour
2 size 2 eggs
1 teaspoon baking powder

For the sauce
140 ml (¼ pint) single cream
2 tablespoon calvados

Cut the pears into large chunks and place in a heavy bottomed pan with the butter and lemon juice. Stew the fruit gently until soft.

Line the base of a deep 15 cm (6 inch) cake tin with greaseproof paper. Grease and flour the sides. With a slotted spoon, lift two-thirds of the pear chunks from the pan and place in the prepared tin.

Beat the sponge ingredients together until smooth and pour over the pears. Bake in a preheated oven at 190°C/375°F/Gas 5 for 40-50 minutes, or until a cake tester inserted in the centre of the sponge comes out clean.

Remove from the oven and allow to sit for 5 minutes, then invert on to a serving dish.

Meanwhile, liquidize the remaining pears with the cream and calvados and warm the sauce through. Do not allow it to boil.

Remove the paper from the pudding and serve with the cream sauce.

WHISKED SPONGE WITH CREAM AND FRUIT

This is a traditional Cornish recipe and makes a wonderfully light sponge. As the mixture contains no fat the cake is best served filled with cream and berries or jam.

SERVES 4-6

3 size 2 eggs, separated
170 g (6 oz) caster sugar
2 tablespoons very hot water
115 g (4 oz) flour

Grease, flour and line two 22 cm (8 inch) sandwich tins.

Place the egg whites in a large bowl and whisk until stiff. Now add the sugar, a little at a time, and continue whisking until you have a dense meringue. Whisk in the egg yolks one at a time and then whisk in 1 tablespoon of hot water.

Fold in the flour with a metal spoon, then fold in the remaining tablespoon of water.

Divide the mixture between the 2 prepared tins and bake in a preheated oven at 190°C/375°F/Gas 5 for 25-30 minutes. The cake will sink a little as it finishes cooking.

Remove it from the oven and allow to cool for 10 minutes in the tin, then finish cooling on a rack.

Fill with whipped cream and berries, and dust the top with icing sugar.

STRAWBERRIES IN KIR

This simple recipe for marinated berries can be used for all summer fruits either singly or in combination. Serve with crème fraîche, vanilla ice cream or perhaps a slice of lemon pound cake.

SERVES 4-6

275 ml (½ pint) fruity white wine
2 tablespoons crème de cassis
1 kg (2¼ lb) fresh ripe strawberries

Pour the wine and cassis into a bowl, then slice in the prepared strawberries. Chill for 1 hour before serving.

STRAWBERRIES WITH ASTI SPUMANTI

Asti spumanti is a lovely sparkling Italian wine. Buy the sweetest asti available and drink the rest with this luxurious pudding.

SERVES 4-6

**450 g (1 lb) ripe strawberries
about 2 tablespoons caster sugar
1 tablespoon brandy (optional)
1 bottle asti spumanti, chilled
vanilla ice cream**

Slice the hulled berries and place in a glass serving dish. Sprinkle over the sugar and brandy and leave to macerate for 30 minutes or more.

Just before serving, open the chilled wine and pour over sufficient to cover the berries.

Serve at once with vanilla ice cream.

PAVLOVA

This light-as-air pudding is perfect with summer fruit and can be shaped into a heart for a romantic occasion.

SERVES 4-6

**3 large egg whites
175 g (6 oz) caster sugar
1 teaspoon cornflour
1 teaspoon wine vinegar
275 ml (½ pint) whipping cream
fresh raspberries, strawberries or peaches**

Whisk the egg whites with an electric beater until stiff. Add the sugar a third at a time and continue to beat until you have a thick glossy meringue.

Sift the cornflour over the meringue and pour over the vinegar. Fold them in with a metal spoon.

Place a sheet of greaseproof paper on a baking tray and draw a heart about 17.5 cm (7 inches) across. Following the outline, pile the pavlova mixture on to the paper. Hollow the centre slightly.

Bake in a preheated oven at 140°C/275°F/Gas 1 for about 75 minutes. Switch off the oven, open the door and leave until the meringue has cooled.

To serve, whip the cream and pile this and the prepared fruit on top. You can tint the cream pink and arrange the berries to follow the outline of the heart.

LEMON AND LIME YOGHURT COOLER

This light refreshing jelly can be sweet or tart according to taste.

SERVES 4-6

finely grated zest and juice of 2 well scrubbed limes and 1 lemon
115 g (4 oz) caster sugar, or to taste
1 sachet gelatine
3 tablespoons water
600 ml (1 pint) Greek natural yoghurt

Place the juices, zest and sugar in a basin and stir until the sugar dissolves. Sprinkle the gelatine powder over the water and leave to swell. Warm the gelatine mixture until it dissolves, then stir into the lemon mixture.

Leave to cool then whisk in the yoghurt and pour into individual glasses. Chill.

VANILLA POACHED FRUIT

Poached fruit is delicious, and infinitely superior to the stewed fruit of the school canteen. This should not be treated as a poor relation recipe or a way of using up second rate or damaged fruit. Choose unblemished fruit and cut them into even pieces.

A stick of cinnamon, some star anise, or a piece of fresh ginger can be used to flavour the syrup as an alternative to vanilla.

SERVES 4-6

about 1 kg (2¼ lb) fruit
sugar to taste
10 cm (4 inch) piece vanilla pod

Prepare each fruit according to type. Wash and slice rhubarb, peel pears and skin peaches or nectarines. Apricots, greengages and plums will need only washing, though they may be halved if liked.

When poaching rhubarb, place the wet fruit and a little sugar in a pan and cook over a gentle heat until the juice runs. Add extra sugar and water if necessary, plus the vanilla pod. Simmer until the fruit is tender, then scrape the seeds from the vanilla pod, add them to the fruit and discard the pod.

For all other fruit, first make a vanilla syrup. Dissolve 115 g (4 oz) caster sugar in 415 ml (¾ pint) water, add the vanilla pod and simmer for 3-4 minutes. Now add the fruit. They should be just covered by the syrup. Simmer gently until tender. Remove the vanilla pod and scrape out the seeds, returning them to the syrup.

Serve warm or cold with cream.

SUMMER FRUIT BRÛLÉE

This recipe is a favourite with my daughters, Jade and Amber.

SERVES 4-6

900 g (2 lb) mixed summer fruit: raspberries, strawberries, blueberries, etc.
275 ml (½ pint) double cream
275 ml (½ pint) Greek natural yoghurt
light muscovado sugar

Check the berries and remove any leaves or stems. Place in a shallow
ovenproof dish. Beat the cream until it thickens, then beat in the yoghurt.
Spread this over the fruit, making sure the cream touches the edges. Chill
overnight.

Preheat the grill for at least 10 minutes. Sprinkle an even layer of
sugar to cover the cream, then place under the grill. Watch carefully,
turning the dish round so the sugar melts as evenly as possible. The sugar
will not form a complete, shiny layer of caramel, but don't worry about
this.

Allow the dessert to cool, then serve.

ELDERFLOWER AND WHITE WINE JELLY

*If I have no homemade cordial I use Thorncroft elderflower cordial, available from
fine food shops, for this recipe.*

SERVES 4-6

275 ml (½ pint) good white wine
140 ml (¼ pint) elderflower cordial
200 ml (⅓ pint) water
1-2 dessertspoons honey
1 sachet powdered gelatine
450 g (1 lb) small strawberries

Mix the wine and elderflower cordial. Put the water and honey in a
saucepan, sprinkle over the gelatine and leave for 15 minutes.

Warm the pan over a low heat, stirring until the honey and gelatine
dissolve and the mixture is clear. Mix with the wine.

Put the strawberries in a glass serving dish. Pour over the jelly and
leave to set.

WINE JELLY WITH SUMMER FRUITS

This is a beautiful pudding. Summer fruit is suspended in clear white wine jelly,
sweetened with honey.

SERVES 4-6

3 tablespoons lemon juice
2 tablespoons clear honey
275 ml (½ pint) white wine
1 sachet gelatine powder
3 tablespoons water
¼ ripe melon
2 peaches
225 g (8 oz) blueberries
2 apricots
115 g (4 oz) raspberries

Mix the lemon juice and honey into the wine, stirring until the honey has dissolved. Sprinkle the gelatine over the water and leave to swell.

Meanwhile, line a 450 g (1 lb) loaf tin with cling film and arrange the prepared fruit as decoratively as possible to fill the tin.

Warm the gelatine slightly and, when it has completely dissolved, stir it into the wine mixture. Pour this carefully over the fruit and cover the top of the dish with film.

Chill until set. Unmould to serve and remove the film.

TIRAMISU

Quite why this delicious trifle of coffee sponge and mascarpone cheese is called pick-me-up I can't imagine. It is so rich that only a few mouthfuls can wipe you out. If you have a sweet tooth add extra sugar to taste.

SERVES 4-6

225 g (8 oz) mascarpone cheese
1 tablespoon caster sugar
a few drops vanilla essence
140 ml (¼ pint) whipping cream
140 ml (¼ pint) very strong coffee
2 tablespoons brandy or coffee liqueur
1 packet sponge finger biscuits
¼ teaspoon cocoa powder

Whisk the cheese with the sugar and vanilla essence. Beat the cream until it is the same consistency as the cheese and fold the two together.

Mix the coffee and brandy or liqueur in a bowl. Dip each biscuit into the coffee mixture and lay in the base of an oblong serving dish to cover. Spread half the cream mixture on the biscuits and then cover with another layer of dipped biscuits. Spread the remaining cream over the biscuits and smooth the surface. Sift on the cocoa powder and leave to set overnight.

BRANDY CROISSANT PUDDING

Leftover croissants, milk, eggs and a little brandy are all you need for this fabulously light 'bread-and-butter' pudding.

SERVES 4-6

butter
2-3 day-old croissants
1 tablespoon chopped mixed peel (optional)
1-2 tablespoons brandy
60 g (2 oz) caster sugar
2 size 2 eggs
415 ml (¾ pint) creamy milk
½ teaspoon vanilla essence
granulated sugar

Butter an ovenproof dish generously. Slice the croissants and arrange in the dish. Sprinkle on the peel. Beat together the brandy, sugar, eggs, milk, and vanilla essence, and strain into the dish.

Allow the pudding to stand for 1 hour. Sprinkle on some granulated sugar and dot with butter, then bake in a preheated oven at 180°C/360°F/ Gas 4 for 45-60 minutes, or until golden brown.

Serve warm with cream.

ZABAGLIONE

This used to be the standard rich finish to a meal in many traditional Italian restaurants. It can be made at home, but has to be served the minute it's ready.

SERVES 4-6

**3 size 2 egg yolks
70 g (2½ oz) sugar
140 ml (¼ pint) Muscat wine**

Put all the ingredients in a round bottomed bowl and whisk together. Put the bowl over a pan of simmering water and with an electric whisk, beat the mixture until it trebles in size and becomes a dense light foam. Remove from the heat and continue to whisk for 1-2 minutes.

Spoon into glasses and serve with sponge finger biscuits.

TRADITIONAL JEWISH CHEESECAKE

Kitty Smulovitch, a reader of my newspaper column, sent me this recipe for cheesecake, which is simply delicious. Follow the instructions carefully and don't worry if some of the crumbs in the crust fall away when you remove it from the tin.

SERVES 4-6

**10 digestive biscuits, finely crushed
450 g (1 lb) curd cheese
140 ml (¼ pint) soured cream
60 g (2 oz) butter, melted
200 g (7 oz) caster sugar
3 tablespoons cornflour
2 size 3 eggs**

Butter a 22 cm (8 inch) loose bottomed cake tin. Tip the biscuit crumbs into the tin. Smooth them round to cover the base and sides, but do not push down.

With an electric beater, mix together the cheese, soured cream, butter and sugar. Slowly beat in the cornflour. Add the eggs and beat until smooth.

Pour this over the biscuits and bake in a preheated oven at 180°C/360°F/Gas 4 for 20 minutes.

The cake will look loose, but don't worry. Allow it to cool and set, then remove it carefully from the tin.

This cheesecake may be served with fruit.

Mocha cheesecake

Rich and luscious, this cheesecake should be served in very small slices.

SERVES 4-6

**200 g (7 oz) plain chocolate digestive biscuits, crushed
60 g (2 oz) butter, melted**

FOR THE FILLING
**250 g (9 oz) ricotta or low fat soft cheese
60 g (2 oz) soft brown sugar
140 ml (¼ pint) soured cream
3 size 2 eggs, separated
2 teaspoons liquid coffee, or 2 tablespoons good instant coffee dissolved
in hot water
115 g (4 oz) plain chocolate, melted
2 tablespoons coffee liqueur (optional)**

Mix the biscuit crumbs with the melted butter. Press to line the base
and sides of a 22 cm (8 inch) springform tin. Chill.

Beat together the cheese and sugar, then beat in the soured cream, egg
yolks, coffee, melted chocolate and liqueur.

Whisk the whites with the caster sugar until the mixture holds soft
peaks, then fold it into the chocolate mixture. Pour on to the base and
bake in a preheated oven at 180°C/360°F/Gas 4 for about 1¼ hours. The
filling will rise slightly and the top may crack, but continue cooking until a
skewer inserted about 2.5 cm (1 inch) from the edge comes out clean.

Allow to cool, then remove from the tin.

TORTEAU DE CHEVRE

This goats cheese 'pie' is found in the Charente and Dordogne regions of France.
'Torteau' is French for turtle and the top of this pie is said to resemble the turtle's
shell.

SERVES 4-6

FOR THE PASTRY
30 g (1 oz) butter
115 g (4 oz) plain flour
1 egg yolk
cold water to mix

FOR THE FILLING
140 g (5 oz) fresh goats cheese
30 g (1 oz) melted butter
60 g (2 oz) caster sugar
½ teaspoon vanilla essence
3 size 2 eggs, separated
60 g (2 oz) plain flour, sifted
½ teaspoon baking powder

To make the pastry, rub the butter into the flour and mix to a stiff dough
with the egg yolk and water. Knead lightly then chill for 15 minutes. Roll
out to fit a deep 17.5 cm (7 inch) ovenproof soup or pasta bowl.

To make the filling, mix together the cheese, butter, sugar and vanilla.
Add the egg yolks and beat them in well. Now add the flour, mixed with
the baking powder. Whisk the whites to a stiff foam and fold the cheese
mixture into them carefully.

Pour the filling into the pastry case and bake in a preheated oven at
220°C/425°F/Gas 7 for 35-45 minutes. The torteau should be well risen
and very dark brown or even black on top.

Remove from the oven and allow to cool.

PEANUT BUTTER AND CHOCOLATE CHIP CHEESECAKE

SERVES 4-6

170 g (6 oz) chocolate digestive biscuits
310 g (11 oz) cream cheese
115 g (4 oz) caster sugar
2 size 2 eggs
1 teaspoon vanilla essence
85 g (3 oz) peanut butter
85 g (3 oz) chocolate chips

Crush the biscuits and press the crumbs into a loose bottomed 17.5 cm (7 inch) cake tin.

In a food processor, whizz the cheese until smooth. Add the sugar, eggs, vanilla and peanut butter and continue to process until well mixed.

Pour the mixture carefully on to the crumbs, then sprinkle on the chocolate chips. They will sink into the mixture.

Bake in a preheated oven at 180°C/360°F/Gas 4 for 45 minutes. Allow to cool, then remove from the tin.

HONEY AND FROMAGE FRAIS TART

Flavouring sweet dishes with herbs dates back to Tudor times, as does baking dishes in pastry 'coffins'. Thyme and honey are delightfully complementary flavours that remind me of Titania's speech in A Midsummer Night's Dream.

SERVES 6-8

22 cm (8 inch) flan tin lined with shortcrust pastry
450 g (1 lb) 8% fromage frais
3 size 2 eggs, beaten
4 tablespoons clear honey
1 teaspoon fresh thyme leaves, crushed

Mix the filling ingredients together and leave for 1 hour to let the flavours infuse.

Line the pastry case with greaseproof paper and baking beans and bake in a preheated oven at 180°C/360°F/Gas 4 for 20 minutes. Remove the beans, pour in the filling and continue to cook, turning down the heat to 150°C/300°F/Gas 2 for a further hour or until the filling is set.

Remove from the oven and allow to cool. Serve at room temperature.

ELDERFLOWER SORBET

The most haunting of summer ices, these delicate elderflower sorbets taste of muscat grapes and gooseberries. The flowers are infused in a sugar syrup, then the syrup is frozen. Serve tiny balls of the sorbet in beautiful long stemmed glasses.

SERVES 4-6

**225 g (8 oz) caster sugar
1 litre (1½ pints) water
about 20 clean elderflower heads
juice of 2 lemons**

Make the syrup: dissolve the sugar in the water, and simmer for 5 minutes.

Remove from the heat and add the elderflowers. Leave to steep overnight and then strain the liquid through fine muslin or kitchen paper. Add the lemon juice and freeze, stirring to break up the crystals after about 3 hours.

PLUM AND CINNAMON SORBET

SERVES 4-6

**450 g (1 lb) dark skinned plums
½ sachet gelatine powder
415 ml (¾ pint) water
140 g (5 oz) caster sugar
1 teaspoon ground cinnamon**

Simmer the plums in 140 ml (¼ pint) water until very soft. Rub through a sieve, discarding the skins and stones.

Sprinkle the gelatine powder over 3 tablespoons water and allow to swell.

Put the remaining water into a saucepan with the sugar and heat until the sugar dissolves. Bring to the boil and simmer for 5 minutes. Allow to cool a little, then add the gelatine mixture, stirring until it dissolves. Now add the prune purée and the cinnamon.

Pour into a freezer tray and freeze, beating from time to time to break down the ice crystals. Alternatively, freeze in an electric ice cream churn according to the manufacturer's instructions.

FRESH PINEAPPLE ICE

This simple recipe calls for a very ripe pineapple.

SERVES 4-6

1 ripe pineapple
juice of 1 large lemon
60 g (2 oz) caster sugar

Cut all the peel, eyes and core from the pineapple and put the flesh in a food processor. Add the lemon juice and sugar and process until the fruit is finely chopped and the sugar has dissolved.

Pour into a suitable container and freeze, beating from time to time to break up the ice crystals.

RASPBERRY PARFAIT ICE

Parfait ices are beaten to a foam before they are frozen, so no further beating is necessary.

SERVES 4-6

340 g (12 oz) fresh or frozen raspberries
140 g (5 oz) caster sugar
2 tablespoons water
3 egg yolks
275 ml (½ pint) single cream

Process the raspberries or rub through a sieve to make a smooth purée.

Dissolve the sugar in the water and boil rapidly for 2 minutes. Whisk the yolks in the bowl of a large free-standing mixer. Pour on the hot syrup and whisk constantly to a thick cold foam.

Fold in the single cream and raspberry purée and then pour into a loaf tin. Freeze until very firm. To serve, dip the tin in a bowl of hot water for 15 seconds then invert on to a plate.

GLACE NOUGATINE AU MIEL

A wonderful party dessert, this glace nougatine is based on a French recipe from the famous chef Jacques Pic.

SERVES 8

100 g (3½ oz) blanched almonds
100 g (3½ oz) skinned hazelnuts
60 g (2 oz) butter
4 size 2 eggs
170 g (6 oz) clear flower honey
100 g (3½ oz) shelled unsalted pistachios
600 ml (1 pint) double cream

Place the almonds and hazelnuts on a baking sheet and toast in a moderate oven for about 15 minutes until light golden brown. Allow to cool.

Mix the butter, eggs and honey in a heavy bottomed pan and cook over a low heat, stirring constantly, until the butter melts and the mixture is on the point of thickening. Remove the pan from the heat and stir in all the nuts. Allow to cool.

Whip the cream until it holds soft peaks and stir in the cold honey mixture. Spoon into a 675 g (1½ lb) loaf tin and freeze overnight.

To serve, dip the tin in hot water and invert on to a plate. Cut very thin slices.

PRUNE, ARMAGNAC AND AMARETTI ICE CREAM

I really love these delicious juicy fruit. I once spent three blissful days near Villeneuve-sur-Lot, epicentre of the French prune growing business. I saw the harvest, the drying and the packing of prunes on small farms and in huge factories and I feasted on prunes prepared in every conceivable fashion. Forget Provence, the Lot Valley is where I left my heart, under a plum tree, on a late summer's day.

SERVES 4-6

600 ml (1 pint) double cream
4 size 2 egg yolks
115 g (4 oz) caster sugar
1 teaspoon vanilla essence
2 tablespoons armagnac
115 g (4 oz) ready-to-eat prunes, soaked overnight
6-8 amaretti biscuits, crushed

Put the cream into a saucepan and bring gently to the boil. Beat the egg yolks with the sugar and stir in the vanilla essence. Now add a little hot cream and stir well. Slowly add the remaining cream and then return the mixture to the pan. Cook over a very low heat, stirring constantly, until the mixture thickens slightly. The custard will coat the back of a spoon lightly, leaving a clean line if you run your finger over the spoon.

Strain the custard into a clean bowl, add the armagnac and allow to cool. Churn or freeze in trays until the mixture is almost frozen, beating the tray-frozen cream once or twice.

Drain the prunes, chop the flesh, and remove the pits. Add the prunes and crushed biscuits to the ice cream, then spoon into a tray and put in the freezer until needed. Use within one week.

Allow the ice to sit for about 1 hour in the fridge before serving.

Rhubarb and mascarpone ice cream

This ice cream is very rich. Mascarpone cheese is about 50 per cent butterfat and tastes wonderful. I use Champagne rhubarb, but you could substitute crushed strawberries or other summer fruit. The flavour of this ice should be very subtle, echoing the fruit served with it.

Use double cream with the tray method of freezing, single cream if you have an electric churn.

Serves 4-6

225 g (8 oz) mascarpone cheese
60 g (2 oz) caster sugar
140 ml (¼ pint) single or double cream (see above)
½ teaspoon vanilla essence
1 teaspoon balsamic vinegar
115 g (4 oz) poached Champagne rhubarb

Beat the mascarpone with the sugar, cream, vanilla essence and vinegar. Fold in the fruit and freeze. If you have an electric churn, follow the instructions; otherwise freeze in a tray, beating the ice well after about 3 hours. Finish the freezing process and store in the freezer until needed.

PRALINE ICE CREAM

This is a very smooth custard-based ice rich with egg yolks. Add the praline towards the end of the freezing process.

SERVES 4-6

600 ml (1 pint) single cream
5 cm (2 inch) strip vanilla pod
4 egg yolks
1 tablespoon caster sugar
85 g (3 oz) granulated sugar
85 g (3 oz) unblanched almonds

In a heavy-bottomed pan heat the cream with the vanilla pod to boiling point and allow to infuse for 15 minutes. Split open the pod and scrape the seeds into the cream. Discard the pod.

In a bowl, beat the yolks with the caster sugar and a little cream. Add the remaining cream then return to the pan and, stirring constantly, cook over a low heat until the custard thickens and coats the back of the spoon.

Strain the custard into a clean bowl and leave to cool, stirring from time to time.

Meanwhile, place the granulated sugar and almonds in a heavy-bottomed pan and heat until the sugar melts and colours and the almonds toast. Pour on to an oiled tray and allow to become completely cold.

Pour the cooled custard into an ice cream churn and churn until nearly frozen, or pour into a tray and freeze until nearly solid, beating the mixture twice to break down the ice crystals. Just before the ice is fully frozen, crush the praline to a fine powder and fold in. Finish the freezing process and store in the freezer until needed.

Fresh peach ice cream

On the same day that I first tasted real Southern-fried chicken I also helped hand-churn the traditional Fourth of July treat, fresh peach ice cream. My hostess, Tricia, mashed the peaches with the sugar and let them steep for several hours beforehand, giving the ice a wonderful depth of flavour.

Serves 4-6

5-6 very ripe peaches
85 g (3 oz) caster sugar
juice of ½ lemon
275 ml (½ pint) double cream

Place the peaches in a deep bowl and cover with boiling water. Leave for 2 minutes then slip off the skins. Cut the fruit open and remove the stones. Roughly chop the flesh.

Add the sugar and lemon juice and allow to stand for 1 hour. Whip the cream until it just begins to thicken and stir into the fruit.

Freeze in a tray, beating to break down the ice crystals after about 3 hours, or use an electric churn.

Halva ice cream

Halva is an Eastern Mediterranean sweetmeat made from ground sesame seeds, nuts and honey. It is available from delicatessens.

Serves 4-6

600 ml (1 pint) single cream
3 egg yolks
30 g (1 oz) caster sugar
170 g (6 oz) halva
1 teaspoon vanilla essence

In a heavy bottomed pan heat the cream until just below boiling point. Beat the yolks with the sugar and then add a little hot cream. Pour this mixture back into the pan and cook, stirring constantly until the custard thickens. Do not allow the mixture to boil.

Leave the custard in the saucepan until it cools, stirring from time to time to prevent a skin forming.

Put the custard, halva and vanilla essence into a food processor and process until smooth.

Freeze either in a tray, stirring to break up the crystals after about 3 hours, or in an electric ice cream churn, according to the manufacturer's instructions.

SUMMER FRUIT ICE CREAM

*This light and delicious ice cream is made with Greek yoghurt
instead of double cream.*

SERVES 4-6

**450 g (1 lb) ripe summer fruit
caster sugar
275 ml (½ pint) Greek yoghurt**

If using blackcurrants stew them first in a little water then sieve and
discard the skins. Rub raspberries through a sieve and mash strawberries.
Mix the fruits together and sweeten to taste. Now stir in the yoghurt and
pour into a freezer tray. Freeze in the usual manner, beating after about 3
hours to break up the ice crystals.

OLD ENGLISH BROWN BREAD ICE CREAM

SERVES 4-6

**600 ml (1 pint) single cream
10 cm (4 inch) piece vanilla pod
4 size 3 egg yolks
60 g (2 oz) caster sugar
170 g (6 oz) wholemeal breadcrumbs
2 tablespoons soft brown sugar**

Put the cream into a saucepan with the vanilla pod and bring to boiling
point. Turn off the heat and leave for 15 minutes. Now fish out the vanilla
pod and slit it open with a sharp knife. Scrape out all the tiny black seeds
within the pod and stir these into the cream. Discard the pod.

Beat the yolks with the sugar. Reheat the cream gently, then add a few
spoons of the hot cream to the eggs and stir well. Pour this mixture back
into the saucepan. Cook the custard, stirring constantly, over a low heat
until it thickens sufficiently to coat the back of a wooden spoon. The
mixture must not boil. Strain the custard into a clean bowl, cover with film
and cool.

Meanwhile, spread the breadcrumbs on a baking sheet. Sprinkle over
the sugar and toast in a medium oven, stirring from time to time until the
crumbs are very crisp and golden. You may need to break them up so that
they dry evenly. Allow to cool.

Churn the custard until almost frozen. Scrape out into a plastic
container, stir in the cold caramelized crumbs and put in the freezer for a
further 30-60 minutes, or until needed.

HOT CHOCOLATE SAUCE

30 g (1 oz) butter
3 tablespoons cocoa powder
5 tablespoons caster sugar
½ teaspoon vanilla essence
140 ml (¼ pint) natural yoghurt or crème fraîche

Melt the butter in a heavy saucepan and add the cocoa, whisking it in well. Add the sugar and cook for about 30 seconds to dissolve.

Stir in the vanilla essence and yoghurt or crème fraîche and heat to boiling point, whisking constantly. Serve at once.

Nuts or mini marshmallows can be stirred in just before serving.

BUTTERSCOTCH SAUCE

45 g (1½ oz) butter
115 g (4 oz) soft brown sugar
1 tablespoon golden syrup
140 ml (¼ pint) crème fraîche or double cream
½ teaspoon vanilla essence

Melt the butter in a heavy bottomed pan and add the sugar and syrup. Cook, stirring often for 3-4 minutes, until the sugar dissolves. Add the cream carefully and beat into the mixture, then bring to the boil and simmer for a further 3-4 minutes.

When the sauce has thickened and is glossy, cool for a few moments, add the vanilla and serve.

Barbecues, Picnic Food & Summer Drinks

One of the great joys of summer is eating outside. It intensifies not only the flavours and aromas of food, but the appetite itself. This chapter is full of suggestions for moveable feasts. It begins with what Americans call the 'cook-out'.

Imagine the joyful moment when meat and flame first met and our ancestors invented the barbecue. They must have made many of the mistakes that we do today. I'm sure that the embers were often too hot when they started cooking, or the meat caught alight because too much fat dripped into the flames. When you are barbecueing, timing is all.

• The fire must be well constructed and lit in plenty of time to reach the correct heat needed to cook the food.

• Good quality charcoal or briquettes are worth the money, as some of the cheaper barbecue fuels seem to lose all their heat just as you put on the first hot dog.

• Try to calculate how long you will need to cook for and use extra charcoal, stacked around the outside of the fire to feed the central cooking zone when barbecueing joints of meat or whole fish.

• If you are having a very large party it is a good idea to have some coals heating in a separate barbecue and transfer them to the main cooking fire as needed.

• Always allow time for starter fluid to burn off before cooking, and don't use painted or stained wood as this too will taint the flavour of the food.

• When the coals are covered with grey ash but glowing red inside, spread them into an even layer, adding new coals at the edge if needed, and put the grill on to heat.

• Test the fire by holding your hand about 15 cm (6 inches) above the grill. If you can just about keep it there to a count of 10 the heat is about right.

• Cook the thickest foods first, moving them to the outside of the grill as they are done.

• Cook vegetable kebabs after the meat, then use the last of the heat to cook bread, cheese or fruit parcels. And don't forget, before you put the flames out, to toast some marshmallows!

• If you are barbecueing in the countryside or on the beach be very careful of fire hazards. Make sure all the coals are extinguished before you leave the picnic spot, dousing them well with water and covering with earth. Clear up the remains of a fire on the beach.

BARBECUED SKEWERS OF SHELLFISH

These skewers are quick to cook on the outside of the grill and can be nibbled while the main course continues to cook in the middle. Use a mixture of seafood and thread on some vegetables to stretch the more costly ingredients.

SERVES 4

12 plump mussels
12 slices thin-cut, lean streaky bacon
4 scallops with coral
12 jumbo prawns
12 button mushrooms
4 small fresh onions (round bulb spring onions are best)
4 oysters

FOR THE BASTE
2 tablespoons olive oil
1 teaspoon lemon juice
1 clove garlic, crushed
sea salt and black pepper
chopped thyme leaves

Mix the basting ingredients together and leave for 1 hour.

Steam the mussels in a little water until they open, drain and allow to cool. Shell them. Cut the bacon rashers in half to give 24 pieces. If the scallops are large, slice each in half.

Reserving 4 slices of bacon, wrap the mussels and scallops in the remainder; then thread them on to the skewers, alternating with prawns, mushrooms and onions. Don't push the pieces too tightly together. Just before you are going to cook the skewers, open the oysters, wrap in the reserved pieces of bacon and thread one on each skewer.

Brush the kebabs well with the basting sauce and cook over a hot grill until the bacon browns and the shellfish is done.

GRILLED SQUID IN KIWI AND LIME MARINADE

Squid is a delicious seafood too often spoiled by poor cooking that renders the flesh tough and tasteless. The wonderfully sweet flavoured flesh is enhanced by a fruit-based marinade and chargrilling. The kiwi fruit has a magical effect on the squid, tenderizing flesh. Don't marinate for longer than 1 hour, or the squid will become mushy.

SERVES 2 OR 4

1 large or 2 medium squid

FOR THE MARINADE
**1 kiwi fruit, peeled and mashed
juice of 1 lime
2 tablespoons olive oil
sea salt and black pepper
1 small red chilli, chopped (optional)
chopped fresh coriander**

To clean squid, run your fingers under the wings and remove them. Then grasp the body in one hand and the tentacles and head in the other and pull apart. Sever the head from the tentacles just below the eyes and discard the head and intestines. Cut the body open to form a triangle of meat and scrape this with a broad bladed sharp knife to remove all the membranes. Turn the squid over and scrape off the skin and any membrane on that side. You should be left with pure white squid flesh. Peel the wings and tentacles if you intend using them.

Make diagonal cuts in the squid with a sharp knife, scoring the flesh but not cutting through it. Do this in both directions to give a cross-hatched effect. Cut into manageable portions.

Mix the marinade ingredients together and pour over the squid. Leave for 30 minutes.

Grill either on a barbecue or under a well heated grill for 4-5 minutes each side. Serve at once with sauté potatoes and a fresh tomato salad topped with pesto.

Skate wing parcels with oriental seasonings

In this recipe, skate moves a long way from the chip shop. The succulent strands of fish that pull away from the gelatinous bones of a skate wing make it easy to eat, an important consideration if you are dining by candlelight in the garden.

As with all delicate fish, skate must be carefully cooked and putting it in a parcel of greaseproof paper or foil keeps in all the flavour and moisture. The parcels can be baked in the oven or cooked on a barbecue, and would make a delicious main course after hot grilled vegetables.

SERVES 4

4 wings of skate
sea salt and black pepper
½ red pepper, very finely sliced
1 leek or 2 spring onions, very finely sliced
1 medium carrot, very finely sliced
chilli oil
soy sauce
Thai fish sauce
juice and finely grated zest of 1 lime

If you intend to cook the parcels over a barbecue, use foil to wrap the fish; otherwise use greaseproof paper. Cut the foil or paper into 4 x 30 cm (12 inch) circles and oil them lightly.

Wash and dry the skate and season lightly with salt and pepper. Divide half the vegetables between the 4 circles and place a piece of fish on top of each. Now put the remaining vegetables on top of the fish, and season each parcel with a few drops of chilli oil and about ½ teaspoon each soy and fish sauce. Add lime juice and zest to taste then fold over the parcels and seal the edges by folding and crimping tightly. This can be done well ahead.

To cook in the oven, place the parcels on a baking sheet in a preheated oven at 200°C/400°F/Gas 6 for 12-15 minutes.

To cook over barbecue coals, make sure that the coals have lost some of their heat. Put the parcels on the grill and cook, giving them a shake from time to time, for about 10 minutes. Carefully unwrap one and test the fish by seeing if it flakes easily from the bone.

Serve with rice.

SATAY STICKS

These tasty morsels of pork and chicken are soaked in a spicy marinade and then grilled. Even if you are not planning a barbecue, it's fun to cook the first course over charcoal, to be eaten informally as your guests drink and talk in the garden. The kebabs can also be easily cooked under a household grill.

SERVES 4

450 g (1 lb) lean pork, beef or chicken breast, cubed

FOR THE MARINADE
½ teaspoon powdered cumin
½ teaspoon ground coriander
1 tablespoon soft brown sugar
1 tablespoon Thai fish sauce
1 tablespoon light soy sauce
1 tablespoon vegetable oil

FOR THE SPICY PEANUT SAUCE
115 g (4 oz) dry-roasted peanuts
4 tablespoons lemon juice
½ teaspoon soft brown sugar
1 teaspoon sesame oil
2 plump cloves garlic, peeled
1 shallot, peeled
¼ teaspoon red chilli flakes, or 1 fresh red chilli, seeded
3 tablespoons vegetable oil
3-4 tablespoons warm water

For the marinade, mix all the ingredients together to a thickish paste. With your fingertips, rub the paste into the meat. Allow to marinate in a cool place for 1-2 hours.

Meanwhile, blend all the ingredients for the peanut sauce, except the water, in a food processor. When nearly smooth thin to the desired consistency with the water. Allow to sit for 1-2 hours to let the flavours mellow.

Thread the meat on to skewers and grill over hot coals. Serve with the peanut sauce.

Spatchcock poussin

Poussins are small chickens weighing about 450 g (1 lb). I like to serve this with fresh bread and salad and a summer sauce made by mixing plenty of chopped soft herbs like tarragon, chervil, parsley and chives with crème fraîche.

Serves 4-6

4 poussins
2 tablespoons chopped tarragon
3 tablespoons olive oil
sea salt and freshly ground black pepper

Wash the poussins and with a heavy sharp knife split them open along the backbone. Cut away the backbone. Snip the wishbone in half and open the bird out flat. Run two long skewers through each bird, to keep them flat during cooking. Mix together the tarragon, oil, salt and pepper and brush the birds all over. Cook on the heated barbecue or under a pre-heated grill for about 15 minutes each side, turning from time to time and brushing with oil occasionally. The skin should be golden and the poussins cooked through.

Serve on large plates to allow plenty of room to manoeuvre.

INDIAN BARBECUED CHICKEN

As the meat here is boneless there is no need to precook it before barbecueing. The recipe comes from Satish Arora of the Taj Hotel group and the chicken is marinated in a wonderful mixture of spices, yoghurt and cashew nuts. Serve it with the coconut, tomato and cream sauce below.

SERVES 4

8 pieces boneless, skinless chicken (breast or thighs)

FOR THE MARINADE
275 ml (½ pint) natural yoghurt
2 cloves garlic, crushed
1 tablespoon ground cumin
3 tablespoons lemon juice
4 green cardamom pods, crushed
½ teaspoon chilli powder
2 tablespoons ground cashew nuts
1 tablespoon oil
salt

Cut the chicken into manageable chunks. Mix the marinade ingredients together. Marinate the chicken pieces for at least 1 hour or overnight.

Thread the chicken on to skewers and cook on a barbecue or under the grill for about 15 minutes, turning often and checking that the chicken is cooked through. When the thickest part of the meat is pierced with a skewer, the juices should run clear.

Serve with the sauce below.

COCONUT, TOMATO AND CREAM SAUCE

If you don't have a fresh coconut to hand, you can make coconut milk from solid coconut cream or from powder. Serve this sauce with Indian barbecued chicken (above).

400 g (14 oz) tin chopped tomatoes
¼ teaspoon chilli powder
¼ teaspoon finely ground pepper
60 g (2 oz) butter
140 ml (¼ pint) single cream
140 ml (¼ pint) coconut milk
salt to taste

Mix all the ingredients together in a saucepan and simmer for about 15 minutes, until the sauce is thick and the flavour well blended. Liquidize and serve hot.

BUTTERFLIED LEG OF LAMB

*This is one of the world's most delicious dishes. It's easy to stick to cooking small
pieces of meat on the barbecue and forget that joints are doubly succulent and juicy
with a crisply chargrilled exterior. Lamb lends itself particularly well to cooking over a
grill. It is best served pink, scented with herbs and basted with olive oil.*

SERVES 6-8

2.5 kg (5 lb) leg of lamb
rosemary
garlic
4 tablespoons olive oil
sea salt and black pepper

If you can, get your butcher to bone the leg. If not, proceed as follows.
Take a small sharp knife and cut through the leg until you reach the bone.
Carefully scrape the meat away from the bone, opening it out to a flatish
piece. Lay it skin side down and make some deep slits in the thickest parts
of the meat. Open these out to give roughly the same thickness all over the
piece of meat, so that it will cook evenly.

Take 4 long skewers and stick them through the meat, 2 from each
direction, to make it hold its shape during cooking. Now crush the
rosemary and garlic into the oil and season it with salt and pepper.

Brush the meat with the seasoned oil, making sure that you reach into
all the crevices. Leave for about 10 minutes, then cook on the barbecue.

The meat will take about 20 minutes each side, so make sure the coals
will last long enough. Turn it from time to time, brushing with the
remaining oil.

Serve carved into thin slices with grilled Mediterranean vegetables
and herb-roasted potatoes.

BARBECUED FILLET OF BEEF WITH MUSHROOMS AND HERB BUTTER

It's much easier to cook a whole fillet on the barbecue than steaks, which tend to overcook the minute your back is turned. Make sure the fire is ready and with enough coals to last for about 30 minutes.

SERVES 6-8

1.3-2 kg (3-4 lb) fillet of beef, trimmed
4 tablespoons olive oil
sea salt and black pepper
1 large open cap mushroom per person
herb butter to serve (see page 60)

Brush the fillet all over with oil, season with salt and pepper, and place on the heated grill. Turn the meat, sealing it on all sides,then cook for about 15 minutes.

Brush the mushrooms lightly with oil and grill, skin side down, for 3-5 minutes, depending on size. Place a slice of herb butter in each mushroom cap and cook until it melts. Slice the beef into portions and serve topped with a grilled mushroom.

If anyone wants their meat well cooked, return their slice to the barbecue for a few more minutes.

KEBABS

Cooking small pieces of marinated meat and fish on a barbecue is a good way to feed a crowd, and you can make wonderful kebabs of summer vegetables for non-meat eaters.

There are no real rules for making kebabs, except to use well trimmed meat, and to make sure that you don't overload the skewers. If it's too tightly packed, the meat in the middle won't cook properly.

Thread the meat, fish or vegetables alternately, putting a sprig of herbs or a bay leaf between some of the pieces. Kebabs are also delicious served in pitta pockets with salad and a squeeze of lemon juice.

SOUVLAKI

Even the smallest Greek restaurant has an open charcoal range on which they cook these skewers of marinated lamb.

SERVES 4

675 g (1½ lb) lean lamb, cubed
1 tablespoon olive oil
2 tablespoons lemon juice
1 teaspoon chopped marjoram
1 plump clove garlic, crushed and chopped
sea salt and black pepper
1 large onion, quartered
pitta pockets
lettuce, spring onion and lemon wedges

Place the lamb in a deep bowl. Mix the oil, lemon juice, marjoram and garlic together and season. Pour over the lamb, mix in well and leave to marinate for about 2 hours.

Open the onion into sections and thread on to skewers, alternating with the meat. Cook over a barbecue or under a preheated grill for about 5 minutes each side. Fill pitta pockets with shredded crisp lettuce, onion slices and the cooked kebabs. Serve with lemon wedges.

PINCHOS

Often found in tapas bars, these little pork kebabs can be made on cocktail skewers as canapés or cut a little larger to be served as a main meal.

SERVES 4

450 g (1 lb) lean pork cut into small cubes
½ teaspoon sweet paprika
½ teaspoon ground cinnamon
pinch of freshly grated nutmeg
sea salt and black pepper
1 teaspoon fresh thyme leaves, crushed
2 tablespoons olive oil
Tabasco to taste

Place the meat in a bowl and rub in the dry spices and herbs. Stir in the oil and Tabasco and leave for about 1 hour. Thread on skewers, grill or fry for 5-8 minutes, then serve.

HAMBURGERS

Homemade beefburgers cooked on a barbecue are delicious, and bear no resemblance to the over-processed extended meat patties so often sold as fast food. Serve them with corn relish.

SERVES 4

450 g (1 lb) lean minced beef
½ large mild onion, finely chopped
2 tablespoons double cream or Greek yoghurt
1 tablespoon chopped chives
1 tablespoon chopped parsley
1 small clove garlic, crushed and finely chopped
sea salt and black pepper

Mix all the ingredients together, working them well with your hands. Shape into 4 patties 7.5-10 cm (3-4 inches) in diameter and 2.5 cm (1 inch) thick. Cook on the barbecue for 4-5 minutes each side.

Serve in lightly toasted buns topped with some mild onion and a spoonful of corn relish.

Spicy spare ribs

SERVES 4

1.3 kg (3 lb) pork spare ribs

FOR THE SAUCE
85 g (3 oz) soft brown sugar
3 tablespoons Worcester sauce
3 tablespoons soy sauce
2 tablespoons wine vinegar
1 teaspoon Dijon mustard
½ teaspoon chilli oil or Tabasco to taste
2 cloves garlic, crushed and finely chopped
1 shallot, finely chopped
140 ml (¼ pint) orange juice
140 ml (¼ pint) stock

Wash the ribs and lay them in a large ovenproof dish.

Mix together all the ingredients for the sauce, except the stock adding the chilli oil or Tabasco to taste, pour over the ribs and leave to marinate overnight.

About 1 hour before you want to eat the ribs, pour over the stock and cook in a preheated oven at 180°C/360°F/Gas 4 for 30 minutes. Remove the ribs from the oven and pour the pan juices into a saucepan. Boil, whisking from time to time, until the sauce reduces and thickens.

Finish cooking the ribs on the barbecue, brushing them with the sauce from time to time. They will take about 20 minutes. Serve with plenty of soft bread to mop up the extra sauce.

Potted blue cheese

This is excellent for picnics. If you want the mixture to be more easily spreadable use butter instead of curd cheese.

225 g (8 oz) blue cheese
115 g (4 oz) Cheddar cheese, grated
115 g (4 oz) curd cheese
1 teaspoon mild mustard

Place all the ingredients in a blender or food processor and blend until smooth. Pot into jars and seal. Leave for about 24 hours before eating to allow the flavours to mellow.

CHICKPEA AND MUSHROOM TERRINE

This earthily flavoured pâté is perfect for summer suppers or elegant picnics, and I often serve it with salad as a main course dish for vegetarians.

SERVES 8

**1 large onion, finely chopped
3 tablespoons olive oil
2 plump cloves of garlic, crushed
2 tablespoons ground cumin
450 g (1 lb) small organic or button mushrooms, finely chopped
sea salt and black pepper
3 tablespoons chopped parsley
2 x 400 g (14 oz) tins chickpeas, drained
2 size 2 eggs
1 tablespoon balsamic or sherry vinegar
3 bay leaves**

Fry the onion in the oil until it begins to brown. Add the garlic and cook for a few minutes. Now add the cumin and fry, stirring constantly, for 1 minute. Put in the mushrooms and cook, stirring from time to time, until they have lost almost all their moisture.

Transfer the mixture to a food processor and add all the remaining ingredients except the bay leaves. Process until puréed and well mixed. Line a greased 900 g (2 lb) loaf tin with greaseproof paper, place the bay leaves in the bottom, then spoon in the mixture.

Bake the terrine in a preheated oven at 180°C/360°F/Gas 4 for 40-50 minutes, or until lightly browned. Remove from the oven and allow to cool completely before removing from the tin.

GRILLED GOATS CHEESE

I have eaten this dish in place of the cheese course at many French restaurants.

SERVES 4-6

**2 medium or 1 large medium-matured goats cheese
salad leaves
oil and vinegar**

Check the cheeses to make sure the rind is intact: if not, wrap them in foil. Grill for 5-6 mintues each side, then slice and serve with lightly dressed salad leaves.

GRILLED CAMEMBERT

SERVES 4-6

**1 medium-ripe Camembert in a wooden box
quince or gooseberry jelly
oatcakes**

Remove the wax paper from the Camembert and wrap in foil. Replace it in the box and put on the barbecue grill. The cheese will heat and after 15-20 minutes the box will ignite! Even if the box has not burned away, the cheese will be cooked after this time.

Place the foil on a plate and open carefully. Spoon out the melted cheese and serve with oatcakes and quince jelly.

FELAFEL

Felafel are a Middle Eastern speciality – a traditional fast food. Ground beans or chickpeas are spiced, formed into balls and deep-fried, then stuffed into pitta pockets. The chickpeas should be this year's – check the sell-by date on the packet.

SERVES 4

225 g (8 oz) dried chickpeas
1.2 litres (2 pints) water
1 teaspoon bicarbonate of soda
1 teaspoon salt
1 bunch spring onions, roughly chopped
3 cloves garlic
large handful chopped parsley
rind and juice of 1 lemon
1½ teaspoons ground cumin
1 teaspoon ground coriander
black pepper and cayenne to taste
oil for deep-frying

Soak the chickpeas in the water for 24 hours, then drain. Put them in a food processsor with the bicarbonate of soda and salt. Process for a few moments to break them up, then add the onions and garlic. Continue to process until the mixture resembles breadcrumbs, then add the remaining ingredients and process until everything is well combined, but still nutty in texture.

Let the mixture sit for 30 minutes for the flavours to develop, then shape into balls the size of walnuts and deep-fry. Serve with green salad and warm pitta bread.

BROCCOLI, GREEN PEPPER AND TOMATO FLAN

This wonderfully coloured flan makes a delicious lunch dish but can be a little fragile, so pack carefully if you want to take it on a picnic.

SERVES 6

225 g (8 oz) broccoli florets
30 g (1 oz) butter
2 shallots, chopped
1 green pepper, seeded and finely sliced
340 g (12 oz) firm ripe tomatoes, seeded and sliced
deep 22.5 cm (9 inch) quiche tin lined with shortcrust pastry
415 ml (¾ pint) double cream
4 size 2 eggs, beaten
1 tablespoon chopped parsley
1 tablespoon chopped chives
salt and pepper

Blanch the broccoli florets in plenty of salted water boiling for 2 minutes. Drain and refresh in iced water. Drain well.

Melt the butter and fry the shallots and green pepper until they soften. Arrange all the vegetables in the pastry case.

Beat the cream with the eggs, add the herbs, season and pour over the vegetables.

Bake the flan in a preheated oven at 180°C/360°F/Gas 4 for 50-60 minutes. Serve warm or cold.

CORNISH PASTIES

The perfect picnic food, pasties were originally the fare of tin miners. Sometimes they were filled with meat at one end and jam at the other. Other times they were stuffed with fish. The miners were said to hold their pasties by one end as they ate and then throw the last dusty piece of crust into the corner for 'the spirit of the mine' who would watch over them.

MAKES 6

FOR THE PASTRY
170 g (6 oz) lard
450 g (1 lb) plain flour
1 teaspoon salt
iced water to mix

FOR THE FILLING
1 medium swede, finely sliced
3 medium potatoes, finely sliced
1 medium onion, finely sliced
450 g (1 lb) lean rump or skirt steak, diced
white pepper and sea salt
1 tablespoon butter
egg or milk to glaze

First make the pastry. Rub the fat into the flour and salt until the mixture resembles fine breadcrumbs, then make a dough with water to mix. Knead lightly, then chill for 30 minutes.

Roll out the pastry to give 6 x 17.5 cm (7 inch) circles. Starting with the swede slices, layer the filling, seasoning well with salt and pepper as you go. Dot with a little butter.

Dampen the edges of the pastry and fold up to give a boat shape. Crimp the top to seal well. Make a small slit to allow steam to escape. Brush with egg or milk, then bake in a preheated oven at 180°C/360°F/Gas 4 for 40 minutes. Turn the oven down to 150°C/300°F/Gas 2 for a further 20-30 minutes, until the pastry is golden brown and the filling cooked.

Pasties are delicious served hot or cold with spicy pickles.

BEER BREAD

Another holiday favourite, this bread needs no kneading and no rising. It will not slice tidily, but is very crusty and tastes delicious. It is best served warm.

---

450 g (1 lb) self-raising flour
1 tablespoon each salt and sugar
275 ml (½ pint) pale American beer

Mix everything together until just combined. Shape the dough roughly and place on a well greased baking sheet.

Bake in a preheated oven at 190°C/375°F/Gas 5 for 50-60 minutes.

SOURED CREAM AND CHILLI CORN BREAD

This lovely golden corn bread is spiked with chilli to give it extra zest. It can be served warm with butter, or you can toast slices on the barbecue and then drizzle them with oil. Take it on picnics to eat with cold chicken and ham.

---

115 g (4 oz) plain flour
115 g (4 oz) cornmeal (polenta)
1 tablespoon baking powder
½ teaspoon salt
2 size 2 eggs
1 small green or red chilli, seeded and sliced
225 g (8 oz) sweetcorn kernels
140 ml (¼ pint) soured cream
140 ml (¼ pint) corn oil

Mix the dry ingredients in a large bowl. In a food processor work together the eggs, chilli and corn kernels until lightly chopped. Add the soured cream and the oil, processing until well mixed.

Pour the mixture on to the dry ingredients and mix just enough to combine. Pour into a well greased 900 g (2 lb) loaf tin and bake in a preheated oven at 200°C/400°F/Gas 6 for 30-40 minutes.

FOCACCIA

*This immensely popular olive oil bread is very easy to make and quite delicious fresh,
toasted or lightly fried to make croûtons for a salad.*

---

30 g (1 oz) fresh yeast
½ teaspoon honey
275 ml (½ pint) warm water
450 g (1 lb) strong white bread flour
1 teaspoon sea salt
8 tablespoons fruity olive oil

Cream the yeast with the honey until the mixture becomes liquid. Add the
water, mix well and leave to froth. This should take 10-20 minutes,
depending on how warm the room is.

Put the flour and salt into a large bowl, add 4 tablespoons oil and the
yeast mixture. Mix until the ingredients are combined, then gather the
mixture into a dough. Don't worry if it seems a little dry: the flour usually
works in well.

Turn on to a board and knead for 10 minutes or until smooth. The
dough may become quite sticky as you knead, but don't add any more
flour unless absolutely necessary.

Place in a covered bowl and leave to rise in the warm for about 1 hour
or until well doubled in size.

Knock the dough back and shape it to fit a 32 x 22 cm (13 x 8 inch)
tin, pressing well into the corners. Allow the dough to rest, covered, in a
warm place for 30-40 minutes, to double in size once more. Heat the oven
to 200°C/400°F/Gas 6.

With the handle of a wooden spoon make deep depressions through
the dough at about 5 cm (2 inch) intervals. Drizzle the remaining olive oil
over the dough and sprinkle the top with coarse salt crystals.

Bake in the preheated oven for 25-30 minutes or until golden brown.
The bread should sound hollow when the base is tapped. Allow to cool on
a rack.

Focaccia can be made with many different toppings. You could soften
2 large sliced sweet onions in the last 3-4 spoonfuls of oil and spread these
over the bread before baking. Or you could scatter fresh herbs like
rosemary, oregano or wild garlic over the bread after you have drizzled on
the oil. Alternatively, try scattering shredded mozzarella cheese on the
dough before baking.

Barbecued bread

Freshly baked bread is always delicious, and never more so than when cooked in the open air. The dough is baked on the barbecue after the main meal has been cooked, using up the remaining heat left in the coals and providing a delicious eastern style flat bread, hot off the fire.

Even the smallest child can help shape the prepared dough into ovals before cooking.

450 g (1 lb) strong white bread flour
1 sachet easy-blend yeast
1 teaspoon salt
2 tablespoons vegetable oil
275 ml (½ pint) warm water

Mix all the ingredients together well and knead for about 5 minutes or until you have a smooth, elastic dough. Leave in a warm place for 1 hour to double in size.

About 20 minutes before you are ready to cook, tear off pieces of the dough and shape into ovals about 10 cm (4 inches) across. The dough should be about 1 cm (½ inch) thick.

Allow to rise again, then cook on the barbecue grill, turning once the bread looks puffy and is golden on the underside. Once both sides are brown remove from the grill, split and butter.

SANDWICH FILLINGS

Everyone has their favourite sandwich fillings: here are a few ideas.

HAM AND CHEESE MELT

Gary Rhodes, chef at London's Greenhouse Restaurant, suggests a topping for lightly buttered wholemeal toast. Mix together grated Cheddar cheese with 1 tablespoon each chopped sweet onion and mayonnaise, and 1 teaspoon mustard. Lay slices of ham on the toast, then spread on the cheese mix. Brown under the grill and serve at once.

TOMATO AND MOZZARELLA

My friend Philip Britten drizzles herb flavoured olive oil over country bread. He then makes a sandwich with sliced mozzarella and tomato, coarse salt and basil leaves.

CHICKEN AND MAYONNAISE

David Sharland of the Savoy Grill makes a sandwich with lightly toasted French bread spread with homemade mayonnaise and filled with crisp lettuce, sliced tomato, sliced chicken and finely sliced Gruyère.

CREAM CHEESE AND FRUIT

Spread 2 slices of raisin bread with cream cheese and fill with a mixture of chopped dates, walnuts, apple slices and grapes.

BANANA

Mash a banana with a little sugar and a squeeze of lemon juice, and use it with soft brown bread. Cut the sandwich into 4: the filling runs alarmingly.

THAI CHICKEN AND MANGO

Mix 1 tablespoon chunky peanut butter with a squeeze of lime juice, a dash of Tabasco and pinch each of sugar and salt. Sandwich this with sliced chicken breast, shredded iceberg lettuce and a few slices of fresh mango, between slices of lightly buttered white toast.

MARINATED GOATS CHEESE

Mash 2-3 balls marinated goats cheese with a little of the seasoned oil they are packed in, and use in a toasted granary sandwich with fresh salad leaves such as rocket and lambs lettuce.

BACON AND STILTON OR BLUE BRIE

Toast a wholemeal pitta, split open and butter the inside. Fill with crisply grilled bacon, thinly sliced Stilton or blue Brie and Cos lettuce. Season with black pepper.

TURKEY, ONION AND ORANGE

Fill a white roll with curd cheese, finely sliced smoked turkey breast, mint leaves and orange segments. Season to taste.

CRAB

This suggestion comes from Brian Turner, proprietor of Turner's Restaurant in London. Spread brown bread with yoghurt, and use it to sandwich well seasoned crab meat mixed with a little chopped sweet onion and scattered with crumbled crispy bacon.

ANCHOVY

Antonio Carluccio, proprietor of the Neal Street Restaurant in London's Covent Garden, suggests buttered brown bread filled with the mashed contents of a small tin of anchovies.

PAIN BAGNA

This delicious sandwich comes from the Mediterranean and can be made as small individual rolls or as here, one big family-size sandwich. This sandwich should be pressed down firmly after filling to make sure the flavours meld, so it doesn't matter if it gets squashed in the picnic basket.

SERVES 4

**1 French country loaf
1 clove garlic
1 can tuna in oil
2 tablespoons pitted black olives, sliced
2 hardboiled eggs, sliced
1 small head soft lettuce
1 large tomato, sliced
salt and pepper**

Cut the top off the loaf and scrape out most of the crumbs. These can be used for another purpose.

Rub the garlic over the inside of the loaf and discard. Lightly flake the tuna and spread this, along with about half of the oil, over the bread. Cover with the olives, eggs, lettuce leaves, tomato and salt and pepper.

Drizzle over the remaining oil and press the top back on. Wrap the loaf firmly in foil and if possible place a weight on top. Leave for at least 1 hour before slicing into wedges.

JAMAICAN GINGERBREAD

This marvellously dark and spicy loaf cake keeps well and is delicious eaten thinly sliced and spread with butter.

---

60 g (3 oz) lard
170 g (6 oz) molasses sugar
115 g (4 oz) black treacle
60 g (2 oz) golden syrup
2 size 2 eggs
1 tablespoon dark rum (optional)
225 g (8 oz) self-raising flour
2 level teaspoons ground ginger
1 level teaspoon mixed spice
60 g (2 oz) sultanas
3 pieces stem ginger in syrup, finely sliced

Put the lard, sugar, treacle and syrup in a saucepan and warm until the fat has melted and the mixture is soft.

Beat in the eggs, then fold in the remaining ingredients. Pour the mixture into a greased, floured 675 g (1½ lb) loaf tin and bake in a preheated oven at 180°C/360°F/Gas 4 for 35-40 minutes or until a skewer inserted into the centre of the cake comes out clean. Cool on a rack. Wrap the cake in foil and store for 24 hours before using.

GOLDEN GINGERBREAD

My friend Sue Laing gave me this, her mother-in-law's recipe.

---

170 g (6 oz) butter
225 g (8 oz) soft brown sugar
340 g (12 oz) golden syrup
1 size 2 egg, beaten
275 ml (½ pint) milk
450 g (1 lb) self-raising flour
½ teaspoon salt
1½ teaspoons ground ginger

Put the butter, sugar and syrup into a saucepan and heat very gently for about 10 mintes until everything melts. Cool a little and then beat in the egg and the milk. Mix in the dry ingredients and pour into a large shallow tin 32 x 22 x 5 cm (13 x 8 x 2 inches).

Bake in a preheated oven at 180°C/360°/Gas 4 for 70-85 minutes, or until well risen and firm to the touch. The cake will start to shrink away from the sides of the tin when it is ready.

Allow to cool, then cut into squares and store in an airtight tin. This cake becomes wonderfully sticky if kept for 48 hours.

POPPYSEED POUND CAKE

Poundcakes are rich loaf cakes, particularly suitable for picnics as they are moist and travel well and usually have no sticky icing to attract wasps.

---

60 g (2 oz) poppyseeds
140 ml (¼ pint) double cream
2 tablespoons lemon juice
grated zest of 1 lemon
115 g (4 oz) soft butter
170 g (6 oz) caster sugar
3 size 2 eggs
170 g (6 oz) self-raising flour
1 teaspoon baking powder

Put the poppyseeds in a bowl with the cream, lemon juice and zest and leave to soak for 30 minutes.

Cream the butter with the sugar and, when light and fluffy, beat in the eggs. Fold in the flour, baking powder and then the poppyseed mixture.

Put the mixture into a greased floured 675 g (1½ lb) loaf tin and bake in a preheated oven at 180°C/360°F/Gas 4 for 45-50 minutes or until well risen and golden brown. A skewer inserted in the centre of the cake should come out clean.

Allow to cool on a rack, then store in an airtight tin.

CORNISH HEAVY CAKE

This recipe for a traditional Cornish cake has been sent to me by Audrey Goodere from Helston in Cornwall. This cake is best eaten the day it's made.

---

115 g (4 oz) lard
225 g (8 oz) self-raising flour
85 g (3 oz) granulated sugar
170 g (6 oz) currants
milk to mix

Rub the lard into the flour and then add the sugar and currants. Add about 5 tablespoons milk and mix to a pliable dough. Turn on to a floured board and roll gently into a circle about 18 cm (7 inches) in diameter and about 2.5 cm (1 inch) thick.

Put the dough in the centre of a large baking sheet – the cake will spread as it cooks – and brush the top with milk. Sprinkle with sugar and mark into 12 triangles.

Bake in a preheated oven at 200°C/400°F/Gas 6 for 20 minutes or until golden brown. Allow to cool for 5 minutes on the sheet, then remove to a wire rack.

DATE AND DEMERARA SCONES

These scones freeze well, but are so quick to make you can have them on the table in about 20 minutes.

The secret of making airy well risen scones is to knead lightly and get the scones into a thoroughly heated oven as quickly as possible after you have added the milk.

For a more traditional scone, perfect for serving with jam and clotted cream, omit the dates and substitute granulated sugar for the demerara.

---

225 g (8 oz) plain flour
2 teaspoons baking powder
½ teaspoon salt
85 g (3 oz) butter or block margarine
30 g (1 oz) demerara sugar
60 g (2 oz) pitted, chopped dates
milk to mix

Mix the flour, baking powder and salt together. Rub in the butter or margarine until the mixture resembles fine breadcrumbs, then add the sugar and dates. Mix to a firm dough with milk. You will probably need 5-6 tablespoons.

Turn on to a lightly floured board and knead gently for a moment. Pat into a circle about 2.5 cm (1 inch) thick and slice into triangles. Place the scones on a baking sheet, brush the tops with milk and sprinkle with sugar.

Bake in a preheated oven at 200°C/400°F/Gas 6 for 10-15 minutes.

REAL LEMONADE

A lovely drink that puts squash to shame. For fizzy lemonade use sparkling water to dilute the concentrate.

---

115 g (4 oz) caster sugar
275 ml (½ pint) water
grated zest of juice of 1 well scrubbed lemon

Put the sugar and water in a saucepan and heat until the sugar dissolves. Bring to the boil and simmer for 4-5 minutes. Allow the syrup to cool.

Add the lemon zest and juice and store, covered in the fridge, until needed.

To use: dilute 1-2 tablespoons syrup with iced water.

ICED TEA

2 teaspoons tea leaves
1.8 litres (3 pints) boiling water
3 tablespoons honey
ice, lemon juice and mint leaves

Infuse the tea leaves in the freshly boiled water for 5 minutes, then strain into a clean jug. Sweeten to taste with honey and allow to cool.

Chill and serve in ice-filled glasses with lemon juice and mint.

ICED COFFEE I

4 heaped tablespoons ground coffee
1.2 litres (2 pints) boiling water
sugar to taste
crushed ice
vanilla ice cream

Infuse the coffee in the water for 5 minutes, then strain into a clean jug. Sweeten to taste, then chill until needed.

Serve the coffee in tall glasses with crushed ice, topped with vanilla ice cream.

ICED COFFEE II

4 tablespoons ground coffee
275 ml (½ pint) boiling water
1 litre (1½ pints) chilled milk
vanilla or coffee ice cream

Infuse the coffee in the boiling water for 5 minutes. Strain into a clean jug and chill.

Mix the chilled coffee essence with the cold milk and serve in tall glasses topped with ice cream.

HYPOCRAS

Dating from Tudor times, this syrup makes a spicy base for a white wine cup or can be diluted with chilled mineral water to make a refreshing drink.

225 g (8 oz) sugar
600 ml (1 pint) water
10 cm (4 inch) cinnamon stick
1 dessertspoon green cardamom pods
5 cm (2 inch) piece of peeled root ginger, crushed

Make a sugar syrup by dissolving the sugar in the water and simmering for 4-5 minutes. Add the spices and leave covered for 24 hours to allow the flavours to infuse. Strain into sterilized bottles and seal.

Serve the syrup diluted to taste with white wine or fizzy water.

ELDERFLOWER CORDIAL

This recipe comes from my sister Victoria. Elderflowers are richly scented and add a heady, muscat flavour to summer cooking. This elderflower syrup keeps well if stored in a cold dark place and is delicious diluted with water or wine, or added to summer punches.

1 kg (2¼ lb) sugar
1.8 litres (3 pints) water
2 well scrubbed lemons
2 well scrubbed oranges
about 20 large elderflower heads
60 g (2 oz) citric acid

Make a sugar syrup by dissolving the sugar in the water and boiling for 5 minutes.

Chop the whole fruit into 2.5 cm (1 inch) chunks and place with the dry flowerheads in a large, spotlessly clean ceramic or glass bowl. Pour over the syrup, stir in the citric acid, cover the bowl and leave in a cold dark place for 4 days to infuse.

Strain off the syrup, pour into spotlessly clean bottles and cover.

ORANGE AND PEACH COOLER

This can be diluted with either water or wine, or on very hot days, perhaps a mixture of both.

115 g (4 oz) sugar
275 ml (½ pint) water
3 ripe peaches, roughly chopped
juice of 2 oranges

Place the sugar and water in a pan, stir until the sugar dissolves, then simmer for 4-5 minutes. Cool. Put the peaches, orange juice and syrup in a blender and whizz until smooth.

Strain through a fine sieve into a glass jug. Add ice and top up with chilled mineral water.

STRAWBERRY CRUSH

115 g (4 oz) ripe strawberries
2 tablespoons caster sugar
3-4 ice cubes
275 ml (½ pint) chilled water

Put the strawberries and sugar in a blender and process well. Add some ice and half the water and process until the ice is finely chopped. Dilute to taste with the remaining water.

LASSI

This spiced yoghurt drink comes from Asia and is wonderfully refreshing.

300 ml (½ pint) thick natural yoghurt
1 litre (1½ pints) chilled mineral water
salt or sugar to taste
ground cumin
fresh mint

Beat the yoghurt with a little of the water until smooth, then add the remaining water. Sweeten or add salt to taste. Add some ground cumin. Chill until needed, then garnish with fresh mint leaves.

STOCK SYRUP FOR COCKTAILS

Many cocktails are sweetened with stock syrup, as sugar does not dissolve easily in cold liquids. The syrup can be stored for several weeks in the fridge.

600 ml (1 pint) water
225 g (8 oz) white sugar

Put the water and sugar in a heavy bottomed saucepan and heat slowly until the sugar dissolves. Bring to the boil and boil uncovered for 5 minutes. Allow the syrup to cool, then store in a clean sealed bottle or jar.

PEACH DAIQUIRIS

4 fresh peaches, skinned and stoned
275 ml (½ pint) crushed ice
275 ml (½ pint) white rum
juice of 1 lemon
2 tablespoons sugar syrup (see above)

Put the ingredients in a blender and whizz until everything is finely chopped to an almost frozen mass. Pour into 4 glasses and serve at once.

PINA COLADA

Rich, sweet and quietly heady, this cocktail tastes deceptively harmless.

fresh pineapple juice
sweet coconut cream
white rum
275 ml (½ pint) ice cubes

Whizz all the ingredients in a blender until well mixed and the ice is finely chopped. Pour into 4 glasses and serve at once.

INDEX